DRAWING FIRE

DRAWING

FIRE

THE EDITORIAL CARTOONS OF BILL MAULDIN

Preface by Tom Hanks

Edited by Todd DePastino

Pritzker Military Museum & Library

Chicago, Illinois

Copyright © 2020 by Pritzker Military Museum & Library
All rights reserved.

Published in the United States by Pritzker Military Museum & Library,
104 South Michigan Avenue, Chicago, Illinois.
pritzkermilitary.org.
All images unless otherwise noted are courtesy of the
Pritzker Military Museum & Library.
Back cover: Bill Mauldin, *Untitled [Self-Portrait at Easel]*, c. 1960
(Copyright © c. 1960 by Bill Mauldin. Courtesy of Bill Mauldin Estate LLC.)
Portions of the Introduction are from Todd DePastino, *Bill Mauldin:
A Life Up Front* (W.W. Norton)

Library of Congress Cataloging-in-Publication Data
DePastino, Todd, editor of compilation, author of introduction.
Drawing Fire: the Editorial Cartoons of Bill Mauldin / edited by Todd
DePastino
Chicago: Pritzker Military Museum & Library, [2020]
Identifiers: ISBN 978-0-998-96894-0 (hardcover)
Subjects: Mauldin, Bill, 1921-2003. | Editorial cartoonists—United States. |
Editorial cartoons—United States. | Cartoonists—United States. | Cartoons
and caricatures | American wit and humor, Pictorial. | World War, 1939–
1945—Veterans—United States—Caricatures and cartoons.
LCC NC1429.M428 D73 2020
741.5092

Manufactured in the United States of America

Front and back illustrations: Bill Mauldin
Cover and book design: Roberto de Vicq de Cumptich

First Edition

2 4 6 8 9 7 5 3 1

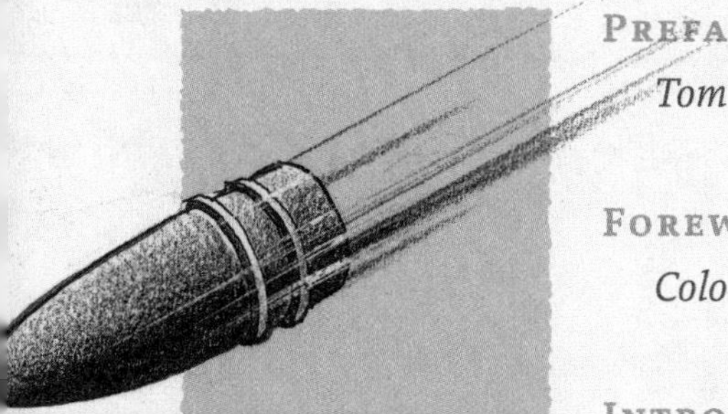

CONTENTS

PREFACE
TOM HANKS

I f a picture is worth a thousand words, Bill Mauldin drew hundreds of novels. Illustrations, comics, panels. Let's call them what they were: dispatches from the front lines of World War II, an indelible record of the misery of its participants and the insanity of its purpose.

"Major Wilson! Back in uniform, I see!"

Willie and Joe—Mauldin's cartoon GIs—take us through a grunt's-eye view of the European Theater of Operations: the mud and cold of their foxhole, the cold rations eaten in the rain, the maddening details of life in the Army, and the physical suffering of soldiering. Willie and Joe were proxy GIs for everyone who could read a newspaper, worry about loved ones in danger, and ponder the global risks at stake in the years 1941 through 1945. The pen of Bill Mauldin provided the laughs, as well as the ironies and the truths, for the duration.

I have two favorite Mauldin cartoons—actually, I have hundreds, but to narrow down the scope of the war years, two stand out.

The day is miserable as a hard rain is falling. An American soldier has his rifle slung barrel down over his shoulder as he slogs through the mud of some war-torn European village. Hungry, ragged, and battle-weary, he is escorting three enemy prisoners of war to their captivity, one with his wounded arm in a sling. With just his pen and black ink, Mauldin captures late-afternoon light, the shadow of defeat, as well as the bone-solid fatigue of the American GI. The caption reads:

"*Fresh, spirited American troops, flushed with victory, are bringing in thousands of hungry, ragged, battle-weary prisoners.*"

Mauldin reported the war as well as any correspondent or observer, taking up only a few square inches of the *Stars and Stripes* to transport the reader to that very day in that very place with those very soldiers. His drawings recorded the war years with fidelity, authenticity, and heart.

My other favorite cartoon is from July 30, 1945—after victory in Europe but before V-J Day and the final end of World War II. Willie and Joe, discharged from the Army and civilians once again, run into their old commanding officer in a big, downtown hotel lobby. The ex-GI's are in nice business suits and ties,

freshly shaven and, well, home. Their former CO, though, is still in a uniform. He's returned to his pre-war occupation as a bellboy.

Genius. Pure and simple. Human and accurate. Bill Mauldin showed the world—and certainly his own subjects, all the Willies and Joes—the common bond that proved they were part of a great generation of Good Americans.

"FRESH, SPIRITED AMERICAN TROOPS, FLUSHED WITH VICTORY, ARE BRINGING IN THOUSANDS OF HUNGRY, RAGGED, BATTLE-WEARY PRISONERS"
(Copyright © 1944 by Bill Mauldin. Courtesy of Bill Mauldin Estate LLC.)

FOREWORD
COLONEL (IL) JENNIFER N. PRITZKER, IL ARNG (RETIRED)

I first learned about Bill Mauldin when I was twelve years old. I come from a family that valued military service, and stories of service were family lore. My grandfathers, Abram Nicholas "A.N." Pritzker and Oscar Gilbert, both served in World War I, as did my great-uncles Harry Pritzker and Wolf Gilbert, along with my great-great-uncle Dr. Louis Pritzker. Those stories inspired me to learn as much as I could about the military, and soon my childhood games shifted to my budding interest in the strategy and history of the armed forces. I was obsessed, reading everything I could in my father's library on the subject. It was there that I came across my father's copy of Bill Mauldin's *Up Front* and the gritty reality of war. Many TV shows and movies I had grown up watching portrayed war as beautiful, glory-filled adventure, but I soon learned the truth. Through Mauldin's work, I discovered that war is not like baseball or any other game. It is painful and mundane, where winning and losing are marked by friends killed, communities destroyed, and lives forever changed. Bill Mauldin's work in World War II illustrated that the enemy isn't so simply defined as evil—he is someone familiar, like you or me, who would rather be anywhere else.

Most important, perhaps, Bill Mauldin opened my eyes to the reality of life in the military. His cartoons do so much more than document the humor of war; in many ways they're also guides for how to succeed in the Army. Because of my early exposure to Bill Mauldin, when I enlisted in the U.S. Army, I was prepared for life both in and out of uniform. The values of a soldier, those of accountability, discipline, control, organization, and comradery, are also those of a leader. Mauldin's understanding of leadership can be seen throughout his books and cartoons, using his own experiences to illustrate the difference between commanders who were loved and those who were loathed. Through Willie and Joe, Mauldin imparts lessons of how to be a successful soldier, what makes a great—and, by comparison, poor—leader, as well

as the value of a morning cup of coffee.

In Mauldin's view, if you want to be a great leader, there are some key attributes that are required. You must look out for the welfare of your troops. You must be competent and fair. You cannot abuse your place of privilege. If you do use any of the privileges garnered to you due to your role, make sure those below understand why you are using them and how it will help the greater good. Be respectful of those above and below you. And never, ever, mess with a soldier's chow, pay, or mail. After the war, Mauldin held those in political leadership roles to the same high standards that he did of officers during the war, lampooning those whom he recognized as falling far short of greatness.

As a Chicago native, my connection to Bill Mauldin has been a lifelong experience. During his time as editorial cartoonist at the *Chicago Sun-Times*, I attended the same school as many of his children. Seeing his cartoons on a regular basis, I was always mesmerized by his ability to confront complex world events with a brush and pen. No one was safe from his scrutiny, as he took on nearly every politician of the day—both foreign and domestic. His cartoons illustrate the political climate and history that my generation experienced; those of us who grew up during the Cold War and the ever-present threat of conflict can look to Bill Mauldin's work and see a timeline of our own lives. Viewed another way, Bill Mauldin's work is a chronicle of the history of the second half of the twentieth century, a history that we in a democratic society all need to understand and appreciate.

It is no coincidence why this collection is so important to the Pritzker Military Museum & Library; the institution was created to acquire and maintain an accessible collection of materials and to develop appropriate programs focusing on the citizen soldier in the preservation of democracy. Bill Mauldin was the quintessential citizen soldier, first volunteering for service to the nation, then returning home to continue his craft by addressing so many of the injustices to help ensure a healthy democracy.

Mauldin took the lessons he learned in the Army, applied them to the world he came home to, and exposed the struggles of civilian life through that lens. Social justice, equality, religious freedom, and tolerance—his ideals and beliefs were shaped by his experiences as a soldier and as a veteran. Whether covering war in Korea, Vietnam, or Israel, he showed that those on the ground still felt the same challenges of service and sacrifice, no matter the era or location. This is what makes his work so special; you can take out the print date or the caption and still see contemporary issues and subjects in his drawings. There is a Bill Mauldin cartoon for every situation, for every topic. With the depth and breadth of his work, there is a Bill Mauldin for everything.

"BEG PARDON. WHICH WAY TO THE FRONT?"
Published on February 6, 1968, this was one of Mauldin's first commentaries on the Tet Offensive, a massive wave of Viet Cong and North Vietnamese attacks that began a week earlier. The Tet Offensive was emblematic of a war without front lines. (Originally published in the *Chicago Sun-Times*, 1968.)

"BEG PARDON. WHICH WAY TO THE FRONT?"

INTRODUCTION
BILL MAULDIN'S WAR, 1921–2003
TODD DEPASTINO

Bill Mauldin's wild fifty-year career defied F. Scott Fitzgerald's oft-quoted remark about there being no second acts in American lives. Mauldin catapulted to fame at age twenty-two as the greatest cartoonist of the Second World War, delivering grim humor from the front lines to newspaper readers back home. After the war, he stunned fans by using his syndicated cartoon as a bully pulpit to protest racial discrimination and anticommunist hysteria. In response to syndicate censorship, he then quit cartooning altogether in 1948. Over the next decade, he wrote articles and books, starred in Hollywood movies, covered Korea as a war correspondent, piloted airplanes, and ran for Congress. In 1958, he went to work for the *St. Louis Post-Dispatch*, won a second Pulitzer prize, then, moving to the *Chicago Sun-Times* in

1962, rose to become one of the nation's most celebrated political cartoonists. Only the *Washington Post*'s Herblock rivaled him in audience and influence. In 2002, near the end of his life, elderly fans, war veterans, returned to pay tribute to Mauldin for his first great act, the one that jolted him from Depression-wracked obscurity to stardom.

Born in 1921 on a remote apple farm in the mountains of southern New Mexico, Billy Mauldin harbored a sense of destiny from the beginning. Almost no one shared it. The child was a prodigy of sorts and could read novels, draw proficiently, and master complex academic tasks at a young age. But in the rural Southwest of the 1920s and '30s, such intellectual prowess counted for little. Billy's strong, handsome, mechanically inclined older brother, Sid, was judged by most to be the better of the two. Billy, on the other hand, was a funny-looking runt who seemed unwilling or unable to carry out the simplest farm chores.

Tuberculosis and rickets had stunted his body, leaving him with a large head and jug ears that stuck out like, he joked, "open doors on a taxicab." Irascible from the day he was born—his grandmother remarked he was the angriest baby she'd ever seen—Billy picked fights with every boy around, from the desert floor in Alamogordo to the top of the mountain in Cloudcroft. He lost all of them. One day, when Billy was ten, he overheard a rancher say, "If that was my kid, I'd drown 'im."

Billy wasn't the only one to bring disrepute on the Mauldin family. His father, whom he called "Pop," had returned disabled from World War I and drove the farm into the ground. Charismatic and unsteady, Pop dragged his family hither and yon in search of the Big Chance: selling wrenches in El Paso, prospecting for gold in Arizona, mining copper in Parral, Mexico. Each venture began with Pop's alcohol-fueled eloquence about the glorious future and ended with the hillbilly family closer to dissolution.

Finally, in 1935, during the sixth year of the Great Depression, things fell apart. Billy's mother left Pop and didn't take the boys. Billy and Sid, ages fourteen and fifteen respectively, decided they were old enough to strike out on their own. They pulled an old Model T from the family junkyard, got it running, and headed to Phoenix, Arizona.

Billy lived on the back porch of a boarding-house and attended Phoenix Union High School as much as he could, though he never graduated. Teachers encouraged his talents and gave him a job as editorial cartoonist on the school newspaper. He earned money painting signs and winning stud poker pots on Saturday night.

Lying in bed on the boardinghouse porch, Billy dreamed of glory. Becoming a famous general or surgeon or preacher—all things he'd entertained as a child—now seemed out of the question. He needed to make a fast strike with his most promising asset: his left drawing hand. He'd read in *Popular Mechanics* that cartoonists like Chic Young (*Blondie*) and Milton Caniff (*Terry and the Pirates*) earned $100,000 a year. Cartooning didn't require a lot of expensive schooling. It seemed like the perfect occupation for him. Not only could he make a "pile of dough" from cartooning, but it also fit his temperament. "I was a born troublemaker and might as well earn a living from it," he reasoned.

Knowing he needed *some* training, Bill convinced his grandmother to lend him $500 for one year at the Chicago Academy of Fine Arts—the only art school he knew that accepted high school drop-outs.

He threw himself into life drawing but did his most important work at night, after a full day of classes and an evening of washing dishes at a local restaurant. A young man in a hurry, Bill had committed himself to a grueling regimen of drawing ten original cartoons each night and submitting them to *The New Yorker*, which paid $100 and up for cartoons. Rarely did he get to bed before two in the morning, and often not until four. He kept awake by chain-smoking self-rolled cigarettes. After he finished his "roughs"—high-quality pencil sketches—he bundled them with a return envelope for mailing to *The New Yorker*. Then he opened the return envelope he'd received that day from *The New Yorker* with his rejected drawings. He carefully removed the rejections and placed them in a new envelope addressed to *Collier's*, which paid slightly less than *The New Yorker*. *Collier's* rejections then got sent to the *Saturday Evening Post*, which paid less than *Collier's*, and the *Saturday Evening Post*'s rejections got sent to *Esquire*, and so on, until twenty-five magazines had submission envelopes for mailing. Over the course of one year, Bill drew and submitted more than 2,500 original cartoons. All but a handful were rejected. The only buyer was *Arizona Highways*.

Today, we might cite Malcolm Gladwell's "10,000-Hour Rule" and see Bill's masochistic wee-hour routine as the moment he

"ENGINEER THWORTBOTHEM IS A GOOD MAN, BUT A PROCRASTINATOR!"
Bill drew this cartoon during his frenetic year in Chicago. He knew cars, roads, and the Southwest, and the only cartoons of his that landed with *Arizona Highways* touched on these themes. (Unknown Publisher, ca. 1940.)

achieved mastery of his craft. It also instilled the discipline that allowed him to create cartoons for publication every day, on the fly, in response to ephemeral observations and insights. For the rest of his life, he rarely went to bed without first sketching a half-dozen cartoon ideas.

In the spring of 1940, his grandmother's tuition money ran out, and Bill returned to Phoenix in the hopes of finding work as a commercial artist. Whatever he got wasn't enough for three meals a day or a new suit of clothes, which he desperately needed. A buddy gave him a tip: join the Arizona National Guard, and you'll get food, cloth-

ing, and shelter. The military appealed to Bill ever since the day he sat spellbound on a fence rail along a mountain road watching the 1st Cavalry Division from Fort Bliss parade to summer maneuvers. The trucks and horses, sabers and scabbards, campaign hats and guidons fired his imagination.

As part of the 45th Infantry Division, the Arizona National Guard had its headquarters and Basic Training at Fort Sill, Oklahoma. Bill joined D Company of the 120th Quartermaster Regiment. Life at muddy Fort Sill almost extinguished Bill's flame for Army glory. The Quartermasters was a cesspool of ineptitude and corruption. The men were lazy and slovenly, and the equipment was old and worn out. D Company's officers and noncoms seemed concerned mostly about their gambling, bootlegging, and loan-sharking rackets. Whenever Bill tried to shine or show extra effort, he was punished. After scoring the highest in the regiment on an IQ test, he was sentenced to KP.

The only bright part of Bill's Army career was the one afternoon a week he spent drawing cartoons for the *45th Division News*. The paper was a morale-boosting experiment, and Bill's mission with *Star Spangled Banter*, as he called his feature, was to mine for humor the everyday lives of the division's enlisted men. Bill had plenty of material and used his pen to target the indignities, indiscipline, and chickenshit of life in D Company. Ethnic Indian humor was also a staple, as the 45th Division recruited heavily

" ENGINEER THWORTBOTHEM IS A GOOD MAN, BUT A PROCRASTINATOR!"

among the tribes of Oklahoma, Arizona, and New Mexico. The only recurring character was Joe, a Native American who was incapable of using the first-person singular.

Star Spangled Banter matured, and the humor deepened in 1941, with Bill's transfer to the infantry, K Company of the 180th Infantry Regiment. The Quartermasters was cushy but dispiriting. The Infantry was tough but inspiring. Bill's company was loaded with Choctaws from Oklahoma, and they took enormous pride in soldiering. They turned out crisply at reveille, cared for their weapons, and didn't pilfer, harass, or run illegal side hustles.

Infantry pride crept into *Star Spangled Banter*, displacing crude ethnic humor. Indian Joe lost his pidgin dialect. The cartoon soldiers stood taller and spoke with more command. The illustrations grew more refined, filled with meticulous renderings of the accoutrements of soldiering, as if striving to reflect the infantrymen's lives back to them. Every detail, every gesture had to be just right. "If a drawing lacked authenticity," Bill later explained, "the idea behind it became ineffectual, too. This was especially true in the infantry, where a man lived intimately with a few pieces of equipment and resented seeing it depicted inaccurately."

Bill's cartoons made him a star in the 45th Division, especially after Pearl Harbor, when civilian audiences suddenly clamored for Army-themed humor. George Baker's *The Sad Sack* and Dave Breger's *Private Breger*

became funny-paper hits, and Bill tried to cash in on the new interest. For the most part, he failed to break through to noninfantry readers. Even *Yank* magazine, the Army's own weekly, rejected his roughs. His cartoons were too niche, too focused on grizzled and dedicated footsloggers. Most of the men pouring into the Army were draftees, neophytes to military life. They were civilians first and soldiers second, in the Army but not of it. For them and their families, *The Sad Sack* was funnier than anything Bill had to offer. Bill's soldiers weren't sad sacks or wide-eyed recruits. They had already bridged the distance from hearthside to bivouac. Their boots were firmly planted in the mud.

If the war had gone as its American planners expected, the infantry would have

"GOOD GOSH! WILLIE STRUCK OIL"

In the summer of 1941, the War Department held the Louisiana Maneuvers, a massive exercise designed to test the underfunded Army's readiness for war. Bill accompanied the 45th Division to Louisiana, where soldiers still clad in World War I–vintage uniforms often wielded two-by-fours instead of actual machine guns. Two men in seersucker suits and a big Oldsmobile approached Bill and convinced him to produce a souvenir book of cartoons to sell to the troops. Bill drew fifteen cartoons and twenty-five drawings in forty-eight hours for a book he called *Star Spangled Banter*. It cost twenty-five cents and was a hit with the 45th Division, though Bill never saw any royalties or the two men again. (Originally published in *Star Spangled Banter*, 1941.)

played a minor role, and Bill Mauldin would have been remembered, if at all, as a footnote, a cult hero of the 45th Division. The Navy and War Departments didn't expect or want a replay of World War I trench warfare, with masses of men slogging it out on the ground. They saw airpower, mobile armor, and long-range weapons as keys to victory. The hardest ground fighting would be accomplished mostly by elite units, not

"GOOD GOSH! WILLIE STRUCK OIL!"

ordinary infantrymen. Magazines, movies, and bond posters trumpeted the Rangers and Airborne, dashing sailors and glamorous flyers, and always the "gung-ho" Marine Corps. Infantry was the neglected stepchild, hardly ever depicted and rarely celebrated. It got the cast-offs and hand-me-downs, the lowest-rated recruits and the worst rations. Should the burden of victory ever devolve on the infantry, war planners judged, the Allies would be in trouble.

Yet, that's precisely what happened in the fall of 1943, after Bill had shipped overseas with the 45th Division and witnessed his first combat in Sicily. By then, he was a three-striped sergeant and a full-fledged member of the *45th Division News*, an Army correspondent, not a rifleman. The assignment had saved him from combat but burdened him with survivor's guilt the rest of his life. The men he trained with and loved became casualties of war, while Bill enjoyed the privileges and relative safety of the rear. The reprieve from combat redoubled Bill's commitment to keeping his cartoon authentic, which meant spending time with the "dogfaces," as infantrymen were nicknamed, on the frontlines.

The rugged terrain and terrible weather of Italy, which the Allies assumed to be the "soft underbelly of the Axis," neutralized American advantages in air power and bogged the men of the 45th Division and hundreds of thousands of others in World War I trench–like warfare. There were few quick liberations or dramatic breakouts. The Wehrmacht controlled the Allies' progress up the spiny Italian boot, engineering expert rearguard fire that kept dogfaces hunkered in freezing foxholes and mountain dugouts for weeks, even months, with no relief. A scarcity of supplies, coupled with skyrocketing casualties, added to the fiasco. C-rations didn't reach the men in sufficient quantities, leading to malnutrition on the lines. Trench foot was endemic due to the lack of adequate footwear and dry socks. German artillery pounded static positions around the clock, leaving survivors with hollow stares and frozen expressions, as if they were on death row.

The folks back home knew none of this, and official Army publications ignored mention of the infantry's plight. But Bill saw it all: the weary brows and unrecognizing faces, the blown bodies and wrecked villages. By December 1943, his combat cartoons took a grim turn and exploded with expressive brushwork. Contours and shadows deepened, adding texture and volume to the folds of the uniforms, the architecture of the rubble, and the undulations of the mud. The angry, forbidding battlescapes captured in Mauldin's thick-lined, cross-contour drawings were matched by his characters' dour expressions. Bill gave voice to the infantry's many grievances in a barrage of bitter cartoons lampooning the lack of food, clothing, ammunition, reinforcements, and competent battlefield leadership. Perhaps more breathtaking than Bill's attack on Army brass was the fact that he got away with it.

The legend of Bill Mauldin—the infantry's tribune—grew by word of mouth from scant copies of the *45th Division News* passed hand to hand. The Purple Heart Bill received on the frontlines from a mortar shell fragment in the shoulder cemented his credibility and made it more difficult for his adversaries to shut down his operation.

Rear base section commanders particularly hated Mauldin's cartoons because they exposed black market corruption and the injustice in how combat soldiers—who made up a tiny fraction of the American troop presence in Italy—were treated during their rare four-day leaves in Naples. Traumatized dogfaces badly needing rest often ended up in jail, then were sent back up to their mountain foxholes to await their inevitable doom.

Infantry commanders smiled wryly when they saw Mauldin's cartoons, for they experienced the same miserable conditions of their subordinates. Bill's work also attracted the attention of the Army newspaper, *Stars and Stripes*, which fiercely defended its editorial independence and shared Bill's outrage about the neglect of common foot soldiers. Editors in Naples engineered Bill's transfer to the paper, which had the largest circulation of any daily in the world. Bill's feature, now titled *Up Front*, reached American forces almost everywhere. Some commanders tried banning Mauldin's work, Gen. George S. Patton Jr., most famously so.

But other generals protected him. Lucian Truscott, Theodore Roosevelt Jr., and even Dwight D. Eisenhower personally intervened to keep Bill's cartoons running.

On January 15, 1944, millions of home front readers learned of Mauldin's cartoon for the first time. In his weekly column, Scripps-Howard's famous war correspondent, Ernie Pyle, declared Bill "the finest cartoonist the war had produced . . . And that's not merely because his cartoons are funny, but because they are also terribly grim and real."

Pyle's endorsement launched a wave of syndication, book, even movie offers. Mauldin signed on with United Feature Syndicate, and in April 1944, *Up Front* began appearing in hundreds of newspapers back home. The hillbilly from New Mexico was well on his way to becoming a celebrity and millionaire.

Bill Mauldin's emergence as an artist of national importance coincided with two major War Department policy shifts that transformed the way Americans understood the war. The first was to promote rather than ignore the crucial role of the infantry. The war in Italy convinced war planners for the first time that no amount of aerial bombardment or long-range artillery would dislodge the Wehrmacht from its stubborn mountain hideouts. Rather, Italy and Europe as a whole would have to be liberated the hard way, one boot step at a time, with masses of infantry leading the way.

Related to this new focus on ground forces was a liberalized approach to media censorship. Before the Italy invasion, the Roosevelt administration had largely instructed news outlets to downplay or erase altogether any reports of combat horrors or trauma. Now, officials in the Office of War Information and elsewhere worried that this "good news only" attitude to wartime publicity might trigger a revolt of rising expectations. If the enemy is always on the run, and the U.S. is winning every battle, then why is the war lasting so long? The White House wanted to tamp down hopes for quick victory and prepare the American people for a longer war and larger casualty lists. The "terribly grim and real" depictions of Willie and Joe, as Mauldin now called his cartoon dogfaces, were just the antidote needed to sober a naïve public.

FRANCE

"IT'S EITHER ENEMY OR OFF LIMITS."
American infantrymen in World War II encountered devastation wherever they went. The Germans demolished towns as they retreated, while the Allies did the same as they advanced. It was a war of brute force that left Italy looking, in Bill's words, "as if a giant rake had gone over it from end to end." Occasionally, a town escaped ruin. In that case, it would be placed off-limits to dogfaces and reserved for rear-echelon soldiers and high-ranking officers to enjoy. (Originally published in *Stars and Stripes*, 1944.)

The Army bestowed its final seal of approval on Mauldin's work in May 1945. Bill had just won the Pulitzer prize (making him the youngest Pulitzer prize winner in history at age twenty-three). Now he got word of the Legion of Merit. "Mauldin's work," the citation stated, "has made him indisputably the best known and most popular American soldier in the theater."

A month later, Bill returned home to fame and fortune, but also to a wife he hadn't seen in more than two years and a child he knew only from pictures. Ernie Pyle, who had been killed near Okinawa two months earlier, had warned Bill the transition would be difficult. "Beware of success," Pyle had told him. Give away your money, he said, retreat to obscurity. Return to cartooning only when everyone has forgotten about you. Then you'll have a shot at being happy again.

Bill took the advice to heart. His book *Up Front* now topped the *New York Times* bestseller list, and movie studios were offering $50,000 for the film rights. He had trouble keeping track of all his money.

In the face of this success, Bill told his literary agent and United Feature Syndicate manager that he wanted out. "I'm a rookie at being a civilian," he said. He needed time off, a sabbatical, to orient himself to his family and recharge after the harrowing years overseas.

The syndicate manager expressed sympathy, then showed Bill his contract, which called for four cartoons a week until April 1948. Lots of people were making good money off Mauldin, and they weren't about to let him just slip away.

Bill left for Los Angeles, where his wife, Jean, and son, Bruce, had established lives together with friends and routines unfamiliar to him. "I have discovered," he wrote his agent, "that two people who have been living alone and apart for two years, doing pretty much as they damn please, have a hard time getting together." By October, the couple had filed for divorce.

The breakup of Bill's marriage to Jean marked a dramatic change in his cartooning. He began lashing out at all manner of wrongs, beginning with the discrimination he witnessed against Japanese Americans in California. It's as if he needed a battle to fight to overcome his disillusionment. He moved to New York City and joined movements demanding civil rights, free speech, labor recognition, public housing, support for displaced persons in Europe, a strong United Nations, and a warmer alliance with the Soviet Union.

Bill's cartoons battled on behalf of causes that would come to define American life in the postwar era. The same reactionary voices resisting civil rights, Bill found, also clamored loudly for war with Russia, opposed immigration, and accused liberals of being unpatriotic subversives who conspired with Communists. Bill's powerful libertarian streak—one trait that remained consistent throughout his life—expressed itself increasingly against those who would deny free speech, civil liberties, or human rights.

As Bill increased the tempo of his attacks on the Right, newspapers around the country began dropping their subscriptions to Mauldin's syndicated cartoon. By February 1946, he was losing a paper a day. United Feature's editors tried bribing and cajoling Bill into moderating his messages. Nothing worked.

So the syndicate began censoring Bill's drawings and captions as they saw fit, often changing the entire meanings of his cartoons.

The censorship outraged Bill. But he also saw that some of the damage was self-inflicted. "Instead of trying to be clever or subtle," he realized, "I said to hell with everybody and let fly with a sledgehammer, when I should have used a needle. Cartoons are no

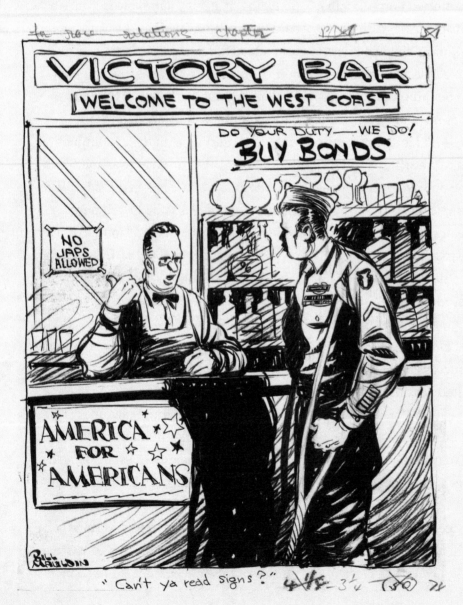

"Can't ya read signs?"

"CAN'T YA READ SIGNS?" This cartoon from September 11, 1945, marked a hard political turn in Bill's postwar work. Here, Bill defends veterans of the Nisei 442nd Regimental Combat Team—the most highly decorated fighting unit in American history—whom he had known in Italy and southern France. Racial segregation and discrimination offended Bill to the core. "It's just that I don't like a man being told he's unequal until he gets a chance to prove his own inequality," he would later say. (Originally published by United Feature Syndicate, Inc, 1945.)

"ABOUT HOLDING UNITED NATIONS CONFERENCES IN YOUR HOME TOWN, SENATOR—YOU MAY ALL BE 100 PERCENT AMERICANS, BUT YOU SEE, UNITED NATIONS INCLUDES OTHER 100 PERCENT NATIONALITIES TOO."

At the end of World War II, the newly formed United Nations was having trouble finding a permanent location. Bill drew this cartoon to express the irony of the UN settling in the land of Jim Crow. United Feature Syndicate changed the caption entirely. Bill's original caption read: "About your proposal to hold United Nations conferences in your home town, Senator—wouldn't the Ethiopian delegation object to riding in the back seats of the busses?" United Feature changed it to: "About holding United Nations conferences in your home town, Senator—you may all be 100 percent Americans, but you see, United Nations includes other 100 percent nationalities too." "I don't think I would have objected quite so strongly had the substitute captions made any sense," Bill said, "but after looking at the horrible things I decided I was not only being censored unmercifully but was being sabotaged as well." (Originally published by United Feature Syndicate, Inc., 1946.)

good if they are soap boxy and pontifical. They have to be thrust gently, so that the victim doesn't know he's stabbed until he has six inches of steel in his innards."

Bill unsheathed his stiletto and regained his balance as a craftsman. He still did battle with the syndicate and racked up some new enemies, including FBI director J. Edgar Hoover, who took personal offense at one cartoon and ordered Mauldin placed under surveillance. In April 1948, his contract expired, and Bill, at the top of his game, walked away from the drawing table.

He was determined to start over. Bill and Natalie, his new wife, settled in a great stone manse thirty-five miles north of Manhattan in Rockland County. The balance of his work shifted from ink brush to typewriter. He worked on novels, screenplays, and television scripts. He published a memoir of childhood titled *A Sort of a Saga* and pitched a dozen other book ideas to his agent. He accepted an offer to star in John Huston's *The Red Badge of Courage* with Audie Murphy. He covered the war in Korea for *Collier's* in 1952. He also learned to fly airplanes, a skill he used to travel on freelance assignments for *Collier's*, *Life*, and *Sports Illustrated*. None of it was steady or added up to full-time work.

A whiskey-fueled meeting with two local Democratic Party officials in March 1956 charged Bill with a new mission. He agreed to run as the party's candidate in New York's 28th Congressional District race against stalwart Republican incumbent (and Franklin Roosevelt's cousin) Katharine St. George. A tough-minded Cold War liberal in the vein of Harry Truman, Bill was no mere celebrity candidate. He immersed himself in the issues and constructed an eight-point platform that included support for Israel, a strong military, civil rights in housing and jobs, and increased aid to public schools and the postal service. He campaigned hard, glad-handing and speechifying sixteen hours a day through a district that stretched across four counties west of the Hudson River. By October, he'd put 15,000 miles on his Piper Tri-Pacer airplane and 20,000 miles on his old Willy's Jeep.

In the end, Katharine St. George won handily, but Bill had performed better in the heavily Republican district than any Democratic candidate ever had. He later said he got as many votes as hands he shook.

The campaign left him and Natalie exhausted and broke. By early 1957, both were looking for another new start. "He was very unhappy," recalled Ralph Martin, his old friend from *Stars and Stripes*. "He couldn't get a focus; he couldn't get an outlet, doing what he really wanted to do."

Martin told Bill that the great Daniel Fitzpatrick, éminence grise of editorial cartooning, was retiring from a fifty-year career at Joseph Pulitzer Jr.'s *St. Louis Post-Dispatch*. Bill campaigned hard for the position, and in March 1958, the paper hired him to the first salaried job he'd ever had. The conditions were severe: his offerings would have to align with the paper's liberal editorial page, or the paper wouldn't print them. There'd be no syndication until later. He'd have to draw six cartoons per week.

The job was a huge adjustment. Gone were the intimate characters, lavish landscapes, and flashing black lines of his earlier drawings. "I had done Willie and Joe in a bold brush, and it was too stark a technique for political cartooning," he said. Instead, Bill worked in pen, crayon, and charcoal, delineating caricatures and visual metaphors in economical shades of gray. "Every line

"ANYTHING RUBBING OFF?"

Bill's new job at the *St. Louis Post-Dispatch* required a looser drawing style with more emphasis on contour and crayon for shading. It also involved him mastering political caricature. Here, Bill expresses his admiration for Dwight Eisenhower while also questioning his judgment in selecting Richard Nixon, a man Mauldin detested, as his vice president. (Originally published in the *St. Louis Post-Dispatch*, 1960.)

©1960 St. Louis Post-Dispatch

"ANYTHING RUBBING OFF?"

and word must justify itself," he said, "otherwise it goes out."

The process of creating a daily cartoon began the night before in bed. Surrounded by newspapers and magazines, Bill sketched six or seven roughs on various topical subjects. The next morning, he took the sketches into a steaming hot bathtub "to boil my brains." The soaking aided his free association, and he emerged from the tub with his day's cartoon concept.

At the office, he sketched a rough for his editor's review. Once approved, the cartoon went back to the drawing table. Using a blunt pencil so as not to get caught up in details, Bill sketched out a half-dozen miniaturized "spots" on typing paper. Each spot took a different approach to composition. He selected a spot, then began the four-hour process of creating the final cartoon. Passersby might hear him talking aloud as he worked, though he interacted with no one. He consulted photo files, reference books, and a Sears, Roebuck catalog if he needed to capture the curl of an arm, the wrinkle of a coat, or the twist of a face. He even had a Polaroid camera with a remote button so he could strike the desired pose himself. Ever the meticulous craftsman, he would go so far as to draw fingernails on his characters, though readers would never see them on a three-column cartoon.

Bill divided his drawing paper into a grid of nine squares and began work from the right bottom corner so as not to drag his left drawing hand over the finished work. He then used a fine-point pen lightly and loosely to go over the pencil marks he'd made, augmenting them further in places with a red sable brush and India ink. Lithographic pencil added shading. Finally, he sprayed the entire drawing with fixative and personally walked it down to the engravers, never trusting anyone else to deliver it. After a couple martinis at a nearby bar, he drove home and began reading for the next day's cartoon.

The exacting regimen paid off. Within weeks, Bill was wielding one of the hottest pens in the business. Six months after coming to the *Post-Dispatch*, Bill drew the cartoon that won his second Pulitzer prize. Other newspapers started trying to lure Mauldin away from St. Louis.

The *Chicago Sun-Times* won the auction for Bill's talents. They almost doubled his salary and syndication royalties. Moreover, they promised him unprecedented freedom to draw as he wished. He'd not have to submit ideas for approval and wouldn't be tied to the tabloid's editorial positions. He'd rove the world as a cartoonist correspondent, serving up visual commentaries on the issues of the day.

The *Sun-Times* sent Bill everywhere there was news. He was in Berlin, for example, when Kennedy delivered his famous *"Ich bin ein Berliner"* speech, and Oxford, Mississippi, when a white mob tried to prevent James Meredith from enrolling at Ole Miss.

His single most memorable cartoon, and

one of the most powerful of the twentieth century, came on his day off, November 22, 1963. He was attending a luncheon at Chicago's Palmer House hotel when a woman stood up and announced that John F. Kennedy had been shot. Bill immediately went to the office. He'd never cared much for the cool, privileged Kennedy, but this was an outrage and his heart turned to the nation in grief. He wondered what kind of drawing he could do to express his feelings. He thought of Lincoln, guessing that, like the 16th President, Kennedy had been shot by an opponent of civil rights. Kennedy was Catholic, so perhaps a religious image might work? But religion always got Bill in trouble, so he cast about for another idea. An editor told Bill he'd have to get the finished drawing to the engravers immediately if he wanted to run in the next edition.

He pulled out a file photo of the Lincoln Memorial and began sketching it as fast as he could. Lincoln's hairline tripped him up. Bill kept drawing Kennedy's hair instead.

"I WON THE NOBEL PRIZE FOR LITERATURE. WHAT WAS YOUR CRIME?"

Only six months into his new career as editorial cartoonist, Bill drew the cartoon that won him his second Pulitzer prize. The news that the Soviet Union banned author Boris Pasternak from traveling to accept his Nobel Prize in Stockholm, Sweden, gave Bill an opportunity to wield his righteous inkbrush for free speech and against oppression without running afoul of the Cold War era's conservative political discourse. (Copyright © 1958 by Bill Mauldin. Courtesy of Bill Mauldin Estate LLC. Image courtesy of the Library of Congress.)

©1963 MAULDIN
Chicago Sun-Times

He wondered if readers would recognize the memorial. But there was no time to perfect it. He sprayed the hastily drawn sketch with fixative and ran it down to the engravers.

Two hours later, the first edition hit the streets. News dealers all over Chicago displayed the tabloid back side up, with Mauldin's cartoon taking up the entire page. The paper sold out in a matter of hours. In the weeks that followed, a half-million requests for copies of the cartoon poured into the *Sun-Times*. The paper issued free reprints, and crowds lined up around the block to get them.

All eyes were on Bill again over a year later when he took off for a tour of the escalating war in Vietnam. His eldest son, Bruce, was in the country, serving as a helicopter pilot in an aviation battalion at Pleiku. Bill was there at Pleiku on February 7, 1965,

UNTITLED [GRIEVING LINCOLN]
Bill's Lincoln Memorial cartoon, states Jules Feiffer, exemplifies his "tragic eloquence." There was a knowledge of tragedy within himself and in his own life, in what he had lived through in the war, before the war, and after the war. He had soul, and it came through in all of the work. (Copyright © 1963 by Bill Mauldin. Courtesy of Bill Mauldin Estate LLC.)

"WHO'S WINNING—THE FORCES OF FREEDOM OR THE PEOPLE'S DEMOCRACIES?"
Bill drew this cartoon shortly before he took off for his trip to Vietnam in early 1965. Bill often depicted the victims of war, those caught in the middle, as a way of exposing the hollowness of sloganeering and high-minded cant. (Originally published in the *Chicago Sun-Times*, 1965.)

"WHO'S WINNING—THE FORCES OF FREEDOM OR THE PEOPLE'S DEMOCRACIES?"

when the Vietcong launched their first major ground attack of the war against American forces. Bill swung into action, patching up and carrying the wounded to a makeshift aid station. As the only reporter on the scene, his dispatches, accompanied by his photos and sketches, brought this critical turning point in the war home to American readers.

Bill had long been skeptical of the American venture in Vietnam, but Pleiku had made the war personal for him. His cartoons grew hawkish. "If we retire from this [battleground]," he said, "[the Communists] will find an even worse one next." President Lyndon Johnson thanked Bill for his support.

Bill's cautious optimism about Vietnam lasted two years. In 1967, his old skepticism returned, especially after his visit to Israel in May of that year. Anticipating that war would soon break out, he embedded himself

WE LOVE MAYOR DALEY

Chicago's Mayor Richard Daley was a favorite target of Mauldin's cartoons beginning in 1968. Mauldin compared him to Mussolini and a pint-sized Keystone Cop. Mauldin held him responsible for the violent attacks on war protesters at the Chicago Democratic National Convention in August and also, as this cartoon suggests, for controlling local press coverage of his administration's malfeasance. In 1969, Bill drew this cartoon not for the *Sun-Times* but for the independent media watchdog the *Chicago Journalism Review*. (Originally published in the *Chicago Journalism Review*, 1969.)

in an Israeli infantry unit overlooking the Sinai Peninsula. There he saw the surprise invasion of Egypt that launched the Six-Day War. He marveled at the Israeli troops' esprit de corps, resourcefulness, and serious-ness of purpose. Working together as one, these citizen-soldiers won a true lightning victory with little of the fancy technology enjoyed by the American military. Bill saw soldiers pick up spent machine-gun casings for reuse. He also detected an utter lack of chickenshit regulations. "I never saw one man salute another," he wrote, "I never saw one man hold a car door open for another. I never saw anybody treat anybody else as a social inferior." In a war of necessity, with national survival at stake, there was no time for the kind of swagger, rhetoric, or jingoism that seemed to infect American military missions. Bill's admiration for the belea-guered Jewish state was so great, his sons began calling him "Lawrence of Israel" upon his return.

Bill had always taken a gut-fighting ap-proach to cartooning. "I'm touchy," he said. "I've got raw nerve ends. . . . If I see a stuffed shirt, I want to punch it. If it's big, hit it. You can't go far wrong." The late 1960s counter-culture encouraged this antiestablishment impulse, and in 1968, Bill's cartoons took a radical turn, winning him a whole new young generation of fans. The countercul-ture also transformed Bill personally.

His youngest son, Nat, noticed the change when he returned from college break and saw his father at the drawing table in his Near North Side studio. Gone was the military hair-cut, the button-down shirt, and the tie. Bill had grown his hair long and, for the first time, sported a beard. Rock music played in the background. On his bed was a young blond woman sitting cross-legged, rolling a joint.

The counterculture may have revitalized Bill's creative work, but it did nothing for his marriage. Natalie and Bill separated, Bill staying on in Chicago and Natalie moving to Santa Fe. He would occasionally fly to New Mexico in his Beechcraft Baron to visit her. In August 1971, Natalie died in a one-car accident while heading to the airport to pick up Bill. Within months, he was engaged to Chris Lund, the cross-legged blonde on the bed. She was twenty-seven years his junior.

The couple moved to Santa Fe, and Bill started his third family. He still cartooned for the *Sun-Times,* and now sent his draw-ings by fax machine. It had, Bill said, "ap-proximately the reproductive capability of a Sicilian copy camera dug from the rubble." The resolution was so poor, Bill returned to his old heavy brush lines with little crayon shading. For the first time, he sacrificed craftsmanship for the comforts and conve-niences of home.

Home included new children. In April 1978, Bill and Chris welcomed the arrival of Kaja, Bill's first daughter. Bill danced down the hallway when she was born, betray-ing his earthy roots by yelling, "It's got no pecker! It's got no pecker!" in celebration.

"What's it like to live with a second-class citizen?"

"WHAT'S IT LIKE TO LIVE WITH A SECOND-CLASS CITIZEN?"

This cartoon from 1977 shows Bill's reversion to heavy brush lines, a result of his reliance on new telefacsimile technology—the fax machine—to get his drawings from Santa Fe to Chicago. Bill was publicly a huge supporter of women's rights and the Equal Rights Amendment, though he tended to treat his wife, Chris, as a second-class citizen at home. (Originally published in the *Chicago Sun-Times*, 1977.)

Kaja was Bill's seventh child from his three marriages. He christened the baby: "Girl One, Litter Three." "Boy Seven, Litter Three," Sam, would follow nine years later.

Shortly before Kaja's birth, Bill finished a book he'd been working on for four years. A cartoon history of the Revolutionary War soldier commissioned by the National Park Service for the Bicentennial, *Mud and Guts* was worth the wait. The project fired Bill's imagination and cast him back to his time in the 45th Division. Bill declared that America was founded by "unlettered, unshaven, sardonic riflemen, whose aim was to get the unpleasantness over and head back to a wilderness full of uncut logs and uncooked game. I had the honor of knowing some of their descendants a couple of centuries later. The offspring weren't much of an improvement, cosmetically speaking, but their attitudes were still healthy—to my way of thinking. I trust they haven't become an endangered species."

Mud and Guts contained the best of Bill's

late career, which began winding down during the Reagan administration. In 1983, he cut back to three cartoons a week. The less he cartooned, the more he was remembered for his wartime work. Veterans began packing his speaking events, waiting patiently for Bill to stop talking about Reagan and El Salvador so they could ask him questions about Patton and Italy. Bill would publish a final collection of cartoons in 1985, *Let's Declare Ourselves Winners . . . and Get the Hell Out*. But he had effectively transitioned from current events commentator to a legacy act, someone valued mostly for his colorful past.

In November 1990, Bill covered his fifth and final war. As the United States prepared to invade Iraq for the First Gulf War, Bill accompanied ABC News reporter Sam Donaldson to visit a half-million troops assembled in Saudi Arabia. Bill's eyes twinkled as he bonded with soldiers young enough to be his grandsons. They had no idea who he was, and Bill didn't care. "I love these guys," he told Donaldson, recalling his own battlefront memories from decades earlier. Bill listened to their gripes about the war and sketched them as they practiced assaults. When he saw some men use upside-down traffic cones to fill sandbags, Bill declared it the greatest innovation in the history of soldiering.

For the war itself, Bill had nothing but disdain. President George H. W. Bush hadn't exhausted peaceful means for settling the conflict with Iraq's Saddam Hussein, claimed

Bill. "Some wars I approve of . . . and some wars I don't approve of," he said, "and I most emphatically do not approve of this one."

The *Sun-Times* fired Bill after he returned from the Middle East. With circulation and profits in decline, a new editor-in-chief explained, Bill's contract was just too expensive. Bill continued to cartoon for his syndicate, mostly to cover the indignity of his humiliating dismissal.

Less than a year later, the day before his seventieth birthday, Bill crushed his drawing hand while working on his old Willys Jeep. Without a job or crusade to focus

"I'M A DISGRACE TO WHAT UNIFORM, SIR?"
Mud and Guts brings Mauldin's famous military humor to soldiers of the Revolution. During WWII, Mauldin's cartoons lampooned officers for their foolhardy obsession with spit and polish. Here, a regular Continental Army officer chastises a citizen-soldier frontiersman who brings only his skill and commitment to the fight to bear on the war, not fancy uniforms or eighteenth-century decorum. (*Mud & Guts: A Look at the Common Soldier of the American Revolution*, 1978.)

"I'm a disgrace to what uniform, sir?"

his energies, he entered a long period of decline marked by infirmities, both physical and mental. Arthritis kept him from drawing or tinkering on his many mechanical projects. Bill's family also noticed changes in his personality. His feistiness and sharp wit turned into irritability, meanness, even paranoia. Chris increasingly became the target of his ire.

Drinking compounded his problems. A teetotaler before World War II, Bill brought the habit home with him, though he wasn't an everyday drinker at first. He was using alcohol to keep his other demons at bay. Then, when drinking itself became a demon, he would quit and abstain for months until the original demons returned. By 1996, when Chris finally began divorce proceedings, Bill's drinking had become a constant, wreaking havoc on his family.

After the divorce, Bill reunited with his first wife, Jean, who cared for him through an agonizing descent into Alzheimer's disease. His incapacity became complete on a horrific morning in 2002. Bill lowered himself into a steaming hot bathtub, as was his long custom. This time, the water was too hot and left him with third-degree burns over two-thirds of his body. Bill survived, but he stopped speaking and seemed not to recognize anyone as he languished in an Orange County nursing home.

Word spread among nearby World War II veterans that the legendary combat cartoonist was in his final days. Aging dogfaces made pilgrimages to his bedside, some in their old uniforms, bearing fragile clippings of their favorite Mauldin cartoons. The news covered the tributes, and mail from around the country poured in with words of thanks from old soldiers. By the time Bill died, more than ten thousand cards and letters had arrived at the nursing home. Mauldin, said one combat infantryman at his bedside, was "the only one who understood us when no one else did."

This tribute, more than any honor or award, ranks Bill Mauldin as one of the greatest artists of the twentieth century.

"My, sir — what an enthusiastic welcome!"

THANK YOU, MR. MAULDIN
TOM BROKAW

I am a child of World War II. My early memories were of life at a U.S. Army Ordnance Depot thrown together on a desolate landscape in southwestern South Dakota, a sprawl of sagebrush, coyotes, and rattlesnakes. It was called Igloo after the earthen bunkers carved into the prairie to protect explosive devices of all kinds shipped up from the mammoth Rocky Mountain Arsenal in Colorado.

Many of these explosive devices were tested on the prairie, so we lived with the regular BOOMS! that rolled across the barracks, tiny cracker-box houses, machine shops, PX, and even a prison compound holding Italian POWs who had been captured and shipped to America.

The business of war was a 24/7 preoccupation. Neighbors were going off to war or coming home on leave. At age three, I wore an Army helmet instead of a regular cap and fought imaginary enemies with toy rifles from the cover of prairie ravines. The base movie theater showed breathless newsreels on American triumphs and profiles of smiling enlisted men and big-name officers.

When the Allies won and the war was over, we moved to a big U.S. Army Corps of Engineers dam construction project on the

"MY, SIR—WHAT AN ENTHUSIASTIC WELCOME!"
(Copyright © 1944 by Bill Mauldin. Courtesy of Bill Mauldin Estate LLC. Image courtesy of the 45th Infantry Division Museum.)

37

Missouri River. Many of the workers were veterans, relieved to be home and almost never referring to their military service.

Then one day a book my mother had ordered arrived. It was called *Up Front* by Bill Mauldin, a boyish enlisted man with a genius for telling the reality of war through his caricatures of Willie and Joe, two weary combat veterans who stripped away the spit and polish, the newsreel facades. They were rumpled, exhausted, bearded fighting men, drawn in bold black-and-white war settings.

I became obsessed with the book and its hard, often hilarious, truths about war from the ground up. Willie and Joe became my companions. I memorized the cartoon captions. One says to the other after racing through a ferocious field of fire, "I made it. I owe ya another fifty bucks." Another had a pompous officer overlooking a valley saying, "Beautiful view! Is there one for the enlisted men?"

That book was my primary connection to the reality of war. In a way, as I thumbed through it again and again, I didn't fully appreciate how Bill and his seminal work spoke to my emerging interest in journalism, or how one can penetrate the superficial and get to essential truths of life in a way that is profound, and that humor is not for laughs alone.

Up Front cartoons had two consistent themes. The first one focused on the brotherhood of Willie and Joe, who personified the reality of life in combat and the shared

sacrifices that came with that. The other Mauldin consistent story line was his disdain for officers whom he portrayed as pompous, pampered elites. He had examples, including one of a general entering a recently conquered village, thinking the locals are welcoming him with fresh fruit when in fact he was being pelted from behind by his own men.

Their disdain for officers was not lost on the legendary Gen. George Patton, the personification of command hubris. He summoned Mauldin for a chewing out.

Imagine you're a cartoonist barely into your early twenties standing before a legendary warrior demanding to know why you characterized officers as out of touch. Mauldin explained to Patton that when the enlisted men open a *Stars and Stripes* newspaper and see a characterization of their gripes they feel validated and therefore less likely to cause trouble.

It was clear Patton didn't agree, but Bill was dismissed without punishment and not long after the meeting he was awarded the Pulitzer prize "for distinguished service by a cartoonist."

He was just twenty-three years old and the war was drawing down.

When I learned more about his hardscrabble childhood in New Mexico and Arizona, I understood Mauldin's commitment to the experiences of all the Willies and Joes, the grunts who take the chances and pay the price.

That comes through even without a caption as Mauldin developed a dark, heavy style that conveyed exhaustion and a kind of weary irony.

Mauldin had been preparing for this assignment since boyhood. Largely unschooled, he learned on the job after joining the 45th Infantry Division in 1940. He served at first as a common soldier before finding a place as a cartoonist on the division's newspaper. A military life, a call to duty, and a passion for the common man all came together in the heart and skills of this gifted young artist.

Years in training, the division finally shoved off for North Africa in June 1943. Then came a major assignment: taking Sicily back from the Germans. It was a two-prong invasion—Great Britain's prima donna Gen. Bernard Montgomery was designated the lead, attacking the eastern rim of the island. Patton was relegated to a supporting role, a slight that infuriated the American general.

In the midst of this major battle, Mauldin and his fellow soldier-journalists had a different objective. They raided local newspapers and printing shops for material to publish for the *45th Division News*. It was in this humble paper's pages that Willie and Joe were born. These characters would soon become emblematic of foot soldiers everywhere.

Mauldin was transferred to *Stars and Stripes*, the military newspaper that broadened his fame to the whole Army. He was given his own jeep, which he drove with reckless abandon from makeshift printing sites to battle sites and first-aid stations. During one of his visits to a company in the thick of a battle, the position came under mortar fire and Bill dove for cover, but he was nicked by a small piece of shrapnel. At the aid station, the doc on duty awarded him a Purple Heart because blood had been drawn. Mauldin's protest was rejected. That medal, along with a Legion of Merit, added to Mauldin's Adjusted Service Rating Score, the "point" system that determined his eligibility to return home after the German surrender in May 1945.

Bill returned from the war and the publication of *Up Front* to an unexpected fame on the home front, prospering beyond his wildest New Mexico schoolboy dreams. He went from a National Guard enlistee to one of the most celebrated young men in uniform. The money poured in from Hollywood, book and magazine publishers, even advertisers.

Reading him now and seeing his postwar cartoons I am struck by the range of Mauldin's social interests. His move from the war front to the home front was seamless and an extension of his "everyman" instincts. His crusade against the immediate postwar automobile market is a piece of history lost in the passage of time. In the years right after V-J Day, the American automobile industry was racing to fill the demands of returning veterans and others eager to replace their prewar models. It was not easy. Mauldin's cartoons about it brought

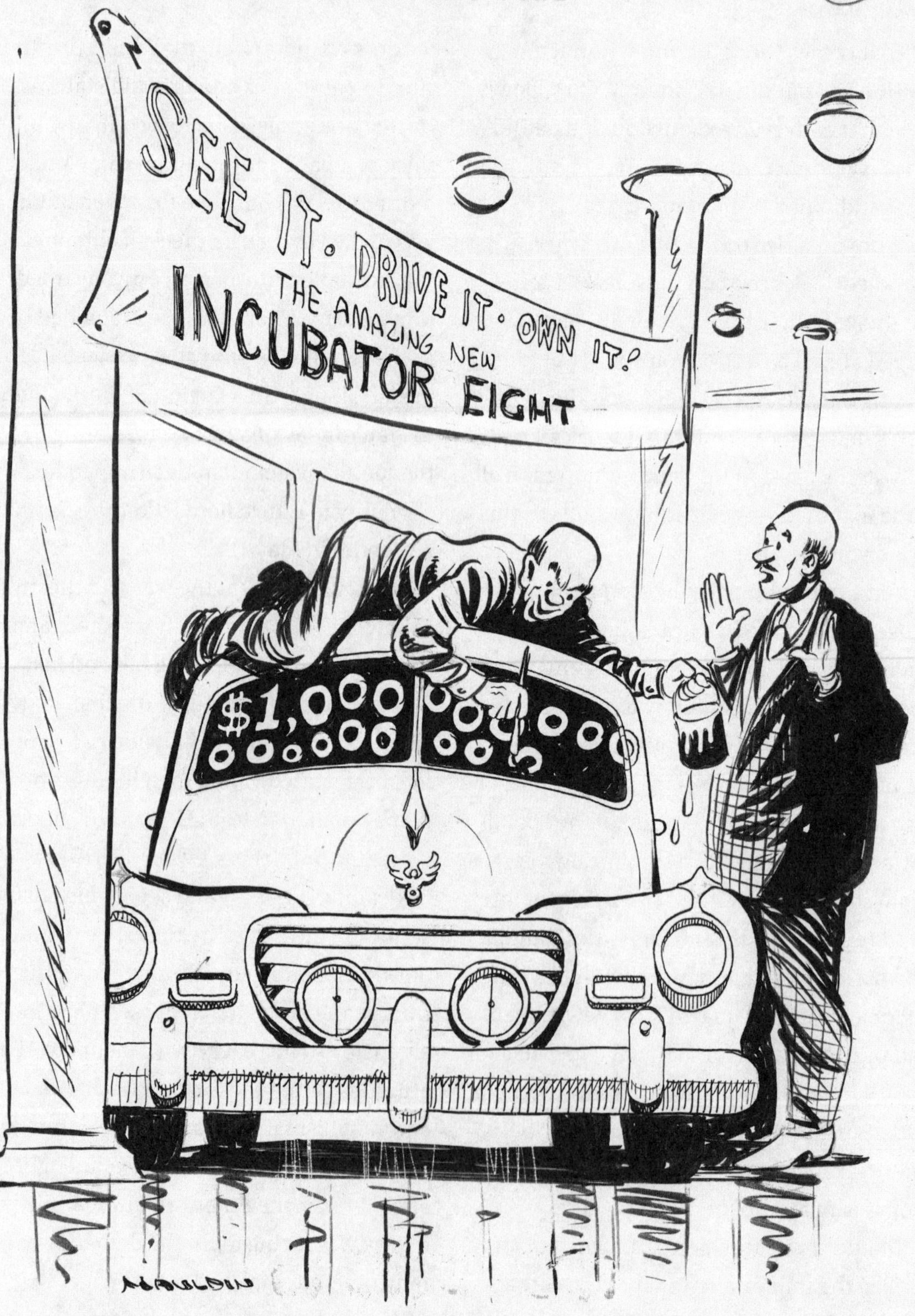
SEE IT. DRIVE IT. OWN IT!
THE AMAZING NEW
INCUBATOR EIGHT
$1,000 000,000,000,000,000
MAULDIN

"Gently, Charlie..."

"GENTLY, CHARLIE . . ."
An automobile fanatic, Bill Mauldin commented much upon the chaotic postwar car market, when new models appeared for the first time since 1942. By July 1946, when this cartoon was published, new car prices skyrocketed dramatically as a result of consumer demand, high wages, materials shortages, and production costs. Inflationary pressures pushed prices up almost weekly, as Charlie's attempt to add more zeroes suggests. (Originally published by United Feature Syndicate, Inc., 1946.)

back to me our family experiences.

My grandparents lost everything in the Great Depression, except their aged Model A car, which by 1946 was about to expire. They had saved enough during the war to pay cash for a 1946 Pontiac sedan. It had all the grace of an armored personnel carrier. It was bereft of styling with a long hood, a boxy body, and an interior that could accommodate eight of my high school football teammates. At least it was new. As Mauldin documented, the used-car market was such an outrageous rip-off, dealers throwing together "bargain" used cars from old taxis and prewar engines, dressing them up with a fresh coat of paint, and promoting them as the pride of the industry.

My dad was a mechanical genius, so he kept our family's 1938 Ford going until the new market car inventory caught up. Even then it was a lottery. By 1950, my parents got on a list for a new Chevrolet sedan, battleship gray, no radio, $1,550 cash.

In his search for a car Bill came across similar vehicles, some of them dressed up by car hustlers who sold them as the new thing in transportation. His own first purchase was $2,500 for a prewar DeSoto with a rigged odometer and a bad paint job that barely covered the bold letters spelling out TAXI on the side.

Now, looking back, I have a renewed appreciation for Mauldin's working-class instincts, which were formed early in that barren New Mexico landscape. He went from looking out for Willie and Joe to looking out in a way for my parents, Red and Jean.

The world of Bill Mauldin was constantly expanding, fueled by his restless curiosity and opportunities he could not have imagined out there on the sage brush landscape of New Mexico. He learned to fly, and his celebrity was a ticket to new friendships that surprised me because I continued to pigeonhole him as a cartoonist.

In Hollywood, he came to know Orson Welles, Burgess Meredith, and the legendary director John Huston. In journalism, he was a pal of two like-minded veterans, Art Buchwald and Andy Rooney. When I shared this with my friend Garry Trudeau, the genius creator of *Doonesbury*, he was surprised because he, too, had confined Bill primarily to the sketch pad. Neither of us was aware he had made a respectable showing as a Democratic candidate for Congress.

Mauldin even starred in a movie, John Huston's *The Red Badge of Courage*, in

1951. Huston twinned him with another southwestern legend from a hardscrabble background, Audie Murphy, a boyish Texan who personally accounted for more than two hundred kills of Germans and became America's most decorated combatant.

Murphy was in another war—he suffered from emotional battles while trying to adjust to a life at peacetime. While working on the film, he dismissed Mauldin as a "faggot" cartoonist and seemed constantly ready to fight.

(A personal note: I was a reporter in Los Angeles when Murphy was called in by Burbank police because a dog trainer claimed Murphy had taken a shot at him while protesting the trainer's treatment of a friend's dog. When Murphy was released a reporter asked if he shot at the trainer. Murphy stared at the reporter and then said, "If I had shot at him, do you think I would have missed?" In 1971, Murphy was killed in the crash of a light plane while scouting movie locations.)

Mauldin decided Hollywood was not for him and returned full-time to his passion: editorial cartooning. It was the era of powerful big-city newspapers owned by equally powerful and wealthy American families. He joined the *St. Louis Post-Dispatch*, which was owned by the Pulitzer family.

He abandoned the heavy lines of his Willie and Joe drawings and worked up a lighter technique for the plethora of subjects in the news: Castro in Cuba, Arab nationalism in the Middle East, and the election of John F.

"IT'S YOUR OWN FAULT FOR ALWAYS SNEAKING AROUND YOUR YARD."

In May 1960, the Soviets shot down a CIA U-2 spy plane piloted by Francis Gary Powers. President Eisenhower's administration at first denied that the United States had been conducting reconnaissance missions in Soviet air space, but Ike was forced to admit the truth when Soviet Premier Nikita Khrushchev produced the damaged U-2 and Powers, who had been captured after ejecting from the plane. In a press conference on May 11, Eisenhower justified the spying by blaming the Soviet Union's "fetish of secrecy and concealment." (Originally published in the *St. Louis Post-Dispatch*, 1960.)

Kennedy and Lyndon Johnson as president and vice president. Bill was back, and his fellow cartoonists took notice. In 1959, he was named Editorial Cartoonist of the Year by the National Cartoonists Society.

Rival newspaper barons took notice as well. Marshall Field IV of the liberal *Chicago Sun-Times* upped the ante: $25,000 a year and royalties, bringing his annual salary to more than $50,000. He was also given a free hand. No editorial approval of his work, and he was encouraged to travel.

When John F. Kennedy was assassinated in Dallas, I was a twenty-three-year-old TV news editor in Omaha on duty when the wire service machines began their frantic clatter signaling a big breaking story. I interrupted a noon time gardening show to break the news and spent the rest of the day trying to cope with the awful magnitude of the murder.

Then a stunning image began to appear.

"IT'S YOUR OWN FAULT FOR ALWAYS SNEAKING AROUND YOUR YARD."

It was the entire back page of the *Chicago Sun-Times*. On deadline in less than an hour, Bill had given the world the perfect, poignant image: Abraham Lincoln, at his memorial, bent over, his head buried in his hands. Mauldin's genius in the darkest of times had given me something to cling to. Bill lost the Pulitzer that year to Paul Conrad, later of the *Los Angeles Times*, who became a close friend when I was posted in Southern California. I never told him I thought Mauldin should have won the coveted prize.

Not surprisingly, Bill lived out his years in a mix of personal turmoil. Too much drinking, a third, much younger wife. The great Sam Donaldson took him along to Desert Shield. It was the precursor to Desert Storm, President George H. W. Bush's war against Saddam Hussein of Iraq, who had invaded neighboring Kuwait. I saw Mauldin there briefly, and he seemed to be on a holiday. The young American soldiers had no idea of his storied background, but he had a helluva good time being back with the troops.

Back home, his health deteriorated. Alcoholism combined with Alzheimer's disease turned him into a sad image of his robust years, far from the gifted poor boy from New Mexico who grew up to give America Willie and Joe, where the foot soldiers, artillerymen, and medics fought the war with a weary sense of duty, humor, and loyalty to one another.

He has a special place in the Greatest Generation and a final resting place at Arlington National Cemetery.

The next time I'm in Washington, I plan to visit his gravesite so I can say, "Thank you, Mr. Mauldin."

"I CAN ALWAYS GET IT BACK INTO THE TUBE."
In the fall of 1990, after Iraq's invasion of neighboring Kuwait, Bill Mauldin accompanied ABC News's Sam Donaldson to Saudi Arabia, where he circulated among the half-million American soldiers staged there for Operation Desert Shield. Mauldin feared that the troop build up would spark a war with Iraq, which could lead the nation into a quagmire comparable to Vietnam. (Originally published in the *Chicago Sun-Times*, 1990.)

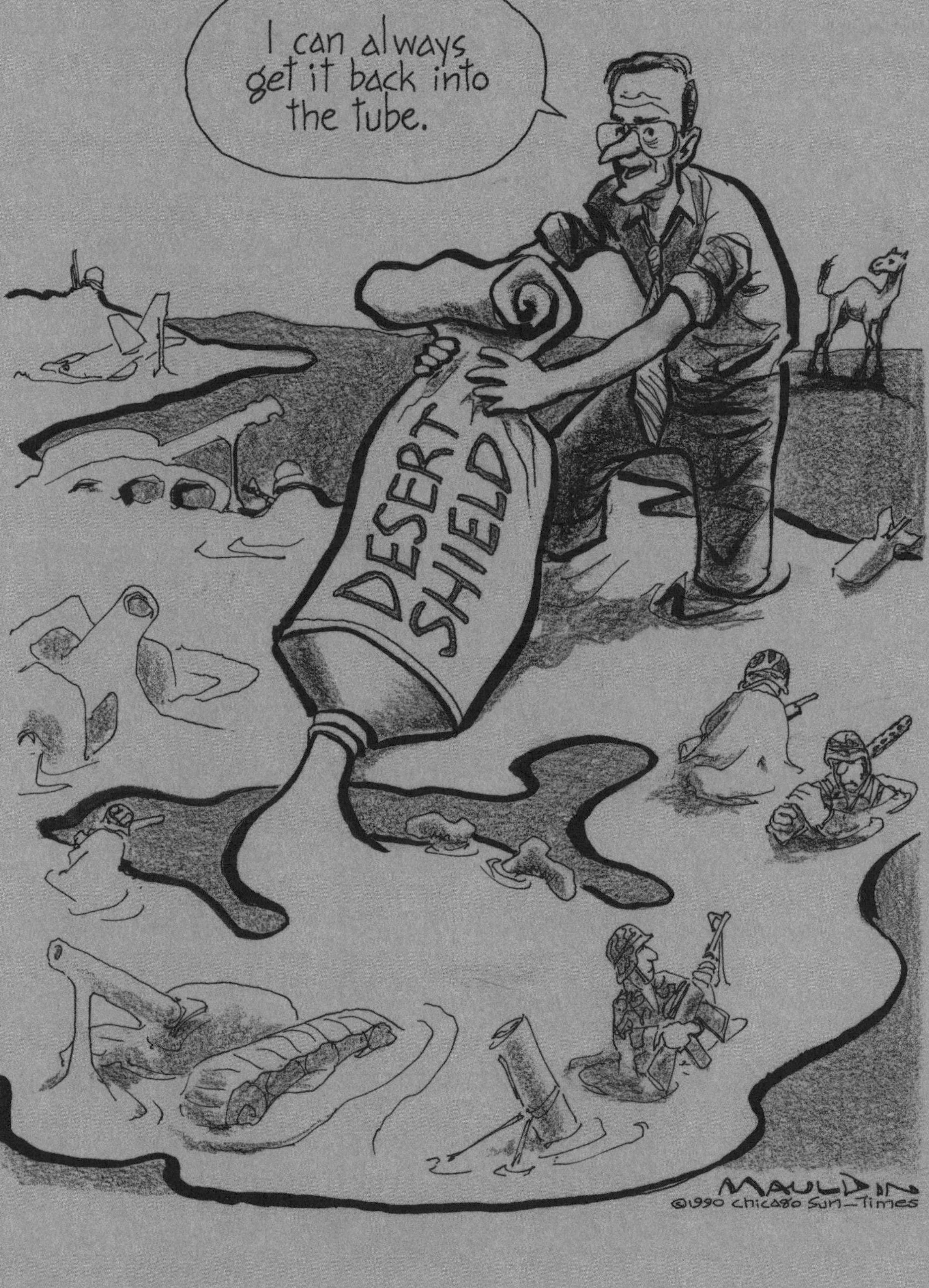
I can always get it back into the tube.
DESERT SHIELD
MAULDIN
©1990 Chicago Sun-Times

BILL MAULDIN, THUNDERBIRD

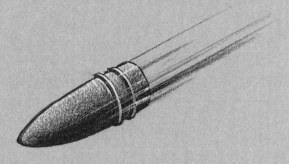

DENISE NEIL

O n the cusp of America's entry into World War II, Bill Mauldin joined the 120th Quartermaster Regiment, 45th Infantry Division. It was a decision that would change the course of his life. Although he had been drawing and cartooning for several years, his time with the Thunderbird Division launched his successful career as a cartoonist. Perhaps it was destiny, or perhaps he was in the right place at the right time; either way, his life in the military became the perfect avenue for using his artistic skills and rapier wit. His early cartoons, produced for the *45th Division News,* were reflections of his own experiences. By the time he left the division to work for *Stars and Stripes*, his drawings had become a voice for the entire infantry. His depictions of Willie and Joe led him to fame, but the time he spent with the 45th Division allowed him to hone his craft as an artist and gadfly.

Wartime training for the 45th Division began at Fort Sill in the fall of 1940. Mauldin's first cartoon in the *45th Division News* appeared in the publication's fourth issue, on October 25. "The Immortal KP" was a single panel drawing featuring a Native American character named Joe. The topic of being placed on KP duty was one that Mauldin had become all too familiar with in the formative days of his military experience. By way of introducing the new cartoon feature, the *News* noted that Mauldin was a good craftsman with a great sense of humor, and, prophetically, "his work with the *45th Division News* may be the start of a fine career."

As the division moved across the United States in preparation for deployment overseas, his popular cartoon series *Star Spangled Banter* reflected the prewar experiences of the men of the 45th. By the time the Thunderbirds participated in the amphibious landing at Sicily in July 1943, Mauldin had proven himself as a capable wartime correspondent. Although a skillful writer, as evidenced by his *45th Division News* feature column "Quoth the

Dogface," it was his ability to capture life in the infantry with strong images and limited text that rivaled the prose of Ernie Pyle's wartime descriptions of the dogfaces.

Many of the cartoons Mauldin created after the division landed at Sicily were observations on the lives and interactions with the Sicilian people. However, it was also during this early fighting that the seriousness of war found its way into Mauldin's renderings. In a drawing featured in the *News* on September 1, 1943, he captured the fighting on Bloody Ridge. There is no humor in this drawing; instead, it records the battle and the mountain fighting that would become all too common for the Thunderbirds. The sketchy line drawing captures soldiers fending off the unseen enemy while other men move supplies up the rugged terrain by pack mule and manpower. Two of the animals have fallen from exhaustion or succumbed to wounds. The theme of mountain fighting and mules would be a subject that Mauldin would return to throughout the Italian campaign.

No words could better describe the situation the dogfaces encountered at Salerno than mud, mules, and mountains, which was appropriately the title of Mauldin's third book. Printed in 1944, it is a collection of cartoons that appeared in the *45th Division News* and his new feature, *Up Front*, in *Stars and Stripes*. This time represents a critical period in Mauldin's career, one in which his cartoons began to record the war through the unique medium of cartooning, and Willie and Joe took on their familiar personas.

Mauldin's final installment of *Star Spangled Banter* appeared in the February 22, 1944, issue of the *News*. His work continued to inspire the Thunderbirds through publication in the *Stars and Stripes*, and now the entire army would have access to his unique wartime perspective. Leaving the 45th Division was not an easy decision. As Mauldin recalled in his autobiography, *The Brass Ring*, "It was a gut wrench to leave the *45th Division News*. We were a bunch of irreverent refugees from line companies with production methods that bordered on buccaneering a good part of the time. The result was a lively, readable, popular newspaper." It seemed joining the military was the most significant career move the cartoonist could have made, and his time with the 45th Infantry Division marked the beginning of his exceptional career.

Mauldin's work was popular among the men of the 45th, but the impact he had during the war, as well as the enduring legacy of his work, was fully realized with *Stars and Stripes*. Humor remains a vital element in Mauldin's work during this period. However, many of his drawings reveal the difficulties and dangers of life on the front lines. Mauldin wrote in *Up Front*, "It's pretty heavy humor, and it doesn't seem funny at all sometimes when you stop to think it over." The exhaustion and fear endured by the dogfaces are captured in many of his most iconic images, including the cartoon, "I can't git no lower, Willie. Me buttons is in th' way." The nighttime battle scene features Willie and Joe in the midst of a firefight. Bullets zing over their heads and artillery shells burst against the dark sky. The caption is filled with the subtle humor that so often wound its way into Mauldin's work, but it is also indicative of the deeper meaning found within his profound images.

Mauldin's career as a cartoonist began as a part-time job working for the *45th Division News,* but the importance of his legacy cannot be overestimated. Today, Mauldin's images continue to resonate with soldiers, but when the body of his work is viewed in its entirety, it paints a historical record of life for the dogfaces in World War II.

"I can't git no lower, Willie. Me buttons is in th' way."

(Copyright © 1944 by Bill Mauldin.

Courtesy of Bill Mauldin Estate LLC.

Image courtesy of the 45th Infantry Division Museum.)

→BACK HOME←
G. KURT PIEHLER

Ernie Pyle and Bill Mauldin were praised by their contemporaries for their ability to understand and interpret the experiences of average GIs who served on the front lines. Both men admired each other's work, with the older and more established Pyle playing a pivotal role in promoting Mauldin's cartoons to the American home front. In the conclusion to *Brave Men,* Pyle speculated about the eventual return of the GIs to their hometowns. He anticipated that there would be a divide between those who had been gone "a long time and . . . have seen and done and felt things you cannot know" and those who remained behind in the States. He predicted these men changed by the war will have to learn how to "adjust themselves to peace." Killed in battle while covering the invasion of Okinawa, Pyle did not have the chance to report on the homecoming and reintegration of GIs back into civilian life. This task was undertaken by Bill Mauldin, who made the reintegration of the fifteen million men and women who served in the armed forces during World War II a major theme of his early post-war cartoons and republished many of them in his bestselling book of 1947, *Back Home.*

Coaxed into joining the National Guard for income, Mauldin might have spent the war as an infantryman, if not for an experiment in GI journalism. Even before Mauldin shipped overseas, his work became a regular feature in the *45th Division News,* and on occasion his cartoons were picked up by local newspapers. In Italy, his cartoons came to the attention of Ernie Pyle and *Stars and Stripes.* By the time he returned stateside, Mauldin had earned a Pulitzer prize, and his cartoons were syndicated and published throughout the United States.

Unlike most GIs, Mauldin returned home not in a cramped troopship, but rather as a VIP passenger in an airplane. The War Department had embraced Mauldin's fame and planned to include him in a military parade in New York City featuring Gen. Joseph Stillwell and honoring the contribution of the infantry. The unexpected departure of Stillwell to take a command in the Pacific led to Mauldin being cut out of the ceremonies accompanying the parade, but not before

he, under the watchful eyes of Army public relations specialists, gave a press conference. Mauldin soon found himself headed to Fort Dix, New Jersey, for his mustering out of the U.S. Army. Eager to return to civilian life and fearful of ruffling any feathers, Mauldin avoided the glare of the press as he waited for his discharge.

Professionally, Mauldin gained much from his Army service—fame, fortune, and plenty of work. His situation was remarkable but not isolated. Other GIs came out of the war with horizons widened. Men such as Dwight Eisenhower, Omar Bradley, and Mark Clark had been colonels in 1939 and emerged from the war as senior generals. While many staffers at *Stars and Stripes* had been civilian journalists, others went on to distinguished postwar careers in the field, such as Andy Rooney and Herbert Mitgang, who had no prior newspaper experience before joining the Army.

In returning home, Mauldin remained quite conscious of his good fortune, beginning with the fact that he managed to serve as a cartoonist with Army newspapers, instead of staying with the infantry. As he wrote in *Up Front*, released shortly after his return home, most older divisions like his own 45th had only a sprinkling of infantrymen who had been with the division since the beginning of their deployment. The rest had been killed or wounded. The syndication of his cartoons had enriched his bank account, and he soon found himself collecting royalties on *Up Front* and garnered a movie deal that paid a $50,000 advance. In contrast to many veterans, Mauldin could pay the exorbitant prices charged for housing and an automobile. The rich and famous wanted to meet him, including former First Lady Eleanor Roosevelt. He found himself receiving invitations to Hollywood parties and to New York's swankiest events.

But Mauldin did not come out of the war unscathed. As with many veterans, years of separation had strained his marriage, and it soon ended in divorce. Although Mauldin had not fought on the front lines, he had witnessed a good deal of death and destruction. He had been in harm's way, often experiencing air raids, artillery barrages, and small-arms fire. His old infantry buddies were largely dead, as were a few of his fellow GI journalists.

After returning to civilian life, the twenty-three-year-old Mauldin sensed that there was nowhere else to go but down. Locked into a contract as a cartoonist with United Feature Syndicate, Mauldin doubted his ability to remain relevant. Eighteen when he enlisted, he had known only the Army for all of his adult life. And he came home to an America that was quite different from the one he had left. Mauldin's first back-home cartoons featured Willie and Joe navigating the transition from soldier to veteran. Then his world expanded. He relocated to New York City and also spent several months living in International Picture Studios in Los Angeles to consult on adapting *Up Front* to a motion picture. Although the movie project would be shelved, Mauldin's time in residence gave him the chance to gauge Hollywood close up. He found the studio system had a hierarchy quite similar to the Army's, with studio executives entitled to a range of perks, including access to the company steam room.

Only two years after returning home, Mauldin published *Back Home*, which contained selections of his most recent cartoons. Part autobiography, part social and political observation, *Back Home* made the bestseller list, though it garnered less of the critical acclaim than his wartime classic, *Up Front*. To this day, *Up Front* has remained in print, even earning a place in the canonical Library of America's two-volume *Reporting World War II*. *Back Home* is an overlooked classic that offers a glimpse of postwar America in flux, a time of contest over the legacy of World War II.

Up Front reflected the censorship of

"AIN'T YOU GONNA BUY A WAR HERO A DRINK?"
Bill Mauldin returned home before V-J Day. His reluctance to wear his uniform or talk about his wartime experiences led many strangers to assume that, because of his youth and civilian clothes, he had avoided military service, and he was subjected to much bravado from home front GIs. (Originally published by United Feature Syndicate, Inc., 1945.)

"Aint you gonna buy a war hero a drink?"

wartime. Mauldin admitted his cartoons only showed part of the reality of frontline combat, beginning with the fact that the dead are never represented. Before going home, Mauldin contemplated killing off his main characters. He abandoned the idea when his editor at *Stars and Stripes* made it clear he would never publish such a dire cartoon. Thus, Mauldin's depiction of combat remained oblique, with the ultimate cost of war only indirectly represented. Frontline soldiers, Mauldin's primary audience for *Up Front*, understood the grim reality they faced and looked to Mauldin for both humor and understanding of their plight, especially when they had to deal with rear-echelon MPs and commanders who harassed them for petty uniform infractions. Infantrymen welcomed his critique of the disparity between the hard life up front and the good living in the rear.

As in *Up Front*, Mauldin is at his best in *Back Home* by remaining detached while still being an empathetic observer of people and events. His initial home front cartoons featured Willie and Joe returning uncomfortably to their families and civilian life. He showed Willie and Joe trying to acclimate to spending time with their children and wives, holding steady jobs, and wearing civilian clothing. In contrast to their wartime appearance, Willie and Joe were clean shaven and properly dressed, often wearing a tie even when shooting pool or playing with children.

Mauldin returned to America while the United States was still at war with Japan, and he offered some keen observations of the American home front. He acknowledged shortages, most notably tobacco products, but contended that the civilian world had little understanding of what long-serving GIs had experienced on the front lines. When one mother expressed dismay that her son had been overseas for months and would not be coming home for some time, Mauldin, who had been deployed overseas for several years, expressed little sympathy for her plight.

On the streets, Mauldin experienced first hand the public suspicion of young men in civilian clothes. People assumed such men were shirkers or draft dodgers. GIs fresh out of basic training or stationed on the home front for the whole war now loudly bragged about their heroic adventures overseas. Mauldin recalled picking up a hitchhiking sailor who started recounting his harrowing time at Anzio and how the Germans were throwing everything at them, including V-bombs. Mauldin, who had been at this beachhead, declined to tell the sailor that V-bombs were never used at Anzio.

"YOU GO AHEAD AN' HAVE A GOOD TIME, POP. I'M TOO TIRED."
The raucous nature of Legion national conventions was legendary during the interwar years. During the 1920s, in the midst of Prohibition, Legion posts in many communities continued to serve alcohol. (Originally published by United Feature Syndicate, Inc., 1945.)

"You go ahead an' have a good time, Pop. I'm too tired..."

THE UNKNOWN SOLDIER

Using the trope of the Tomb of the Unknown Soldier in Arlington National Cemetery, Mauldin sought to capture the plight of returning veterans who needed work, needed a place to live, and sought access to promised benefits under the GI Bill of Rights.
(Originally published by United Feature Syndicate, Inc., 1946.)

"THERE'S JACK O'MALLEY ON HIS WAY HOME FROM THE PACIFIC." ➡

The sudden end of the Pacific War strained the ability of the armed forces and the passenger railroads to bring soldiers from Asia home in an expeditious manner. The loosening of federal government restrictions on civilian travel after V-J Day further compounded the problem.
(Originally published by United Feature Syndicate, Inc., 1946.)

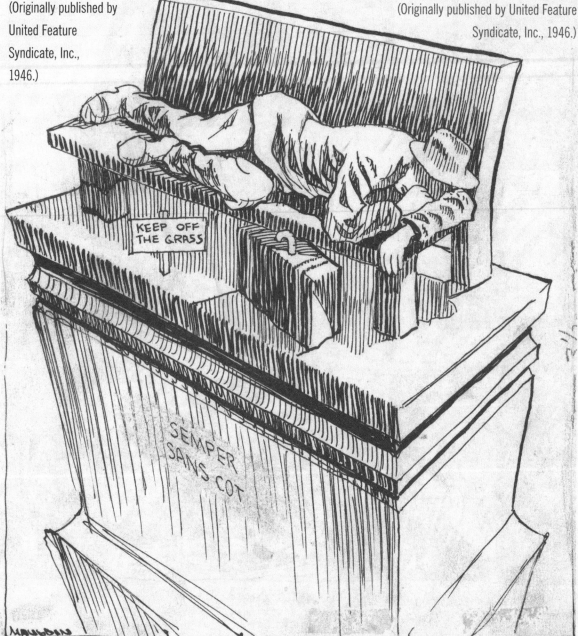

"There's Jack O'Malley on his way [struck out] Union Pacific." 78

"You soldiers just don't seem to understand our problems."

Another continuity between *Up Front* and *Back Home* is Mauldin's delight in finding humor in everyday experiences. As a *Stars and Stripes* cartoonist, Mauldin had acquired a jeep and roamed freely, seeking those on the front line and observing the life of the rear echelon. Fortunate to be able to purchase an automobile and paying top dollar for one, Mauldin roamed the country in his first two years back in the States and changed his residence several times. In *Back Home,* he devoted an entire chapter to the automobile market, in which price gouging, fraud, and shoddy mechanics were the norm.

In *Up Front*, Mauldin was more gadfly than rebel, even when lampooning officers. Indeed, he enjoyed patrons among the senior brass. At the very top, Eisenhower's senior aide, Navy captain Harry Butcher, played a pivotal role in diffusing Gen. George Patton's efforts to suppress Mauldin and *Stars and Stripes.* Mauldin never sought to overturn the established order. He simply wanted infantrymen and combat medics to receive more support from officers and greater recognition for the disproportionate sacrifices they made. There's little by way of idealism or

"YOU SOLDIERS JUST DON'T SEEM TO UNDERSTAND OUR PROBLEMS."

The housing shortage remained severe until the late 1940s. It was exacerbated by the lack of construction during the Great Depression and the war combined with the desire of many veterans to start families. (Originally published by United Feature Syndicate, Inc., 1945.)

ideology in *Up Front.* Willie and Joe fought not for grand ideals, but for each other.

As a soldier, Mauldin avoided politics. Willie and Joe never trumpeted the Four Freedoms or called for overturning Army hierarchy, even while they griped about officers and MPs. As a civilian, by contrast, Mauldin embraced politics and a number of liberal causes, most notably civil rights and the plight of displaced persons. Like many Americans, Mauldin expressed hope in the United Nations and believed Americans should strive to promote a peaceful world. He had a strong disdain for the American Legion, in part because of what he viewed as their hidebound conservatism, juvenile antics at their conventions, and neglect of needs of returning World War II veterans. Although never an activist, Mauldin lent his name to the American Veterans Committee, a new veterans' organization whose motto was "Citizens First, Veterans Second."

Despite newfound wealth, Mauldin remained a keen observer of the average veteran's struggle to readjust to civilian life. *Back Home* complicates the narrative that developed around the Greatest Generation in the 1990s and early 2000s. This narrative portrays the American GI returning home to a grateful nation that bestowed on them a generous set of benefits through the GI Bill of Rights. In this sanguine story, GIs flocked to college and vocational schools that offered them a ticket to the burgeoning middle class. Mortgages underwritten by the GI Bill allowed them to not only attend college or trade school, but also purchase homes in the suburbs, where their children could attend good schools and enjoy the benefits of consumer society.

Mauldin's work bears testimony that most veterans of the "good war" received no welcome-back parades, and in fact, many struggled to return to their hometowns after the federal government lifted controls over the railroads and airlines. In several biting cartoons, railroad companies came under criticism for not allocating more space for returning soldiers eager to get home. So desperate were some GIs, they actually took to hitching rides on freight cars, like hoboes.

Mauldin offered a string of cartoons featuring the plight of veterans in search of decent housing and especially critical of landlords who gouged returning servicemen and, even worse, refused to rent to families with children. Although the United States escaped a postwar depression, Mauldin recounted how the conversion from defense to civilian production did lead to dislocations.

Almost all of Mauldin's overseas cartoons focused on white infantrymen. Few depict minority groups or women. Mauldin merely adhered to the War Department's projection of a lily-white image of war. In *Back Home*, for the first time, Mauldin spoke strongly about racial and religious discrimination. Although Mauldin declared in *Back Home* it would be comforting to believe the war had promoted greater tolerance, plenty of Amer-

icans embraced stereotypes about African Americans, Japanese Americans, and Jews. Some even supported Nazi racial theories.

Mauldin became particularly irate at the discrimination that returning Nisei soldiers endured when they headed to their homes on the West Coast. He recounted that he saw a great deal of them when they fought as a battalion assigned to the 34th Division in Italy and saluted the bravery of these Nisei soldiers from the West Coast and Hawaii who were now being denied service at restaurants and bars. Critical of the white racists who took over Nisei homes, farms, and businesses when second-generation Japanese Americans were overseas or in internment camps, Mauldin also took aim at the William Randolph Hearst newspaper chain for continuing to fan the flame of prejudice against Asian Americans on the West Coast and anti-black sentiment in the South.

When Mauldin's cartoons denounced the racial violence perpetrated by the Ku Klux Klan, several newspapers, North and South, dropped his cartoons. Mauldin particularly skewered the hypocrisy of northern liberals who bemoaned the travails of African Amer-

"NAW—WE DON'T HAFTA WORRY ABOUT TH' OWNER COMIN' BACK. HE DIED IN ITALY."
Mauldin underscores the injustices committed to Japanese Americans; so many had not only endured internment, but were unable to recover lost businesses, farms, and homes in their old communities. (Originally published by United Feature Syndicate, Inc., 1945.)

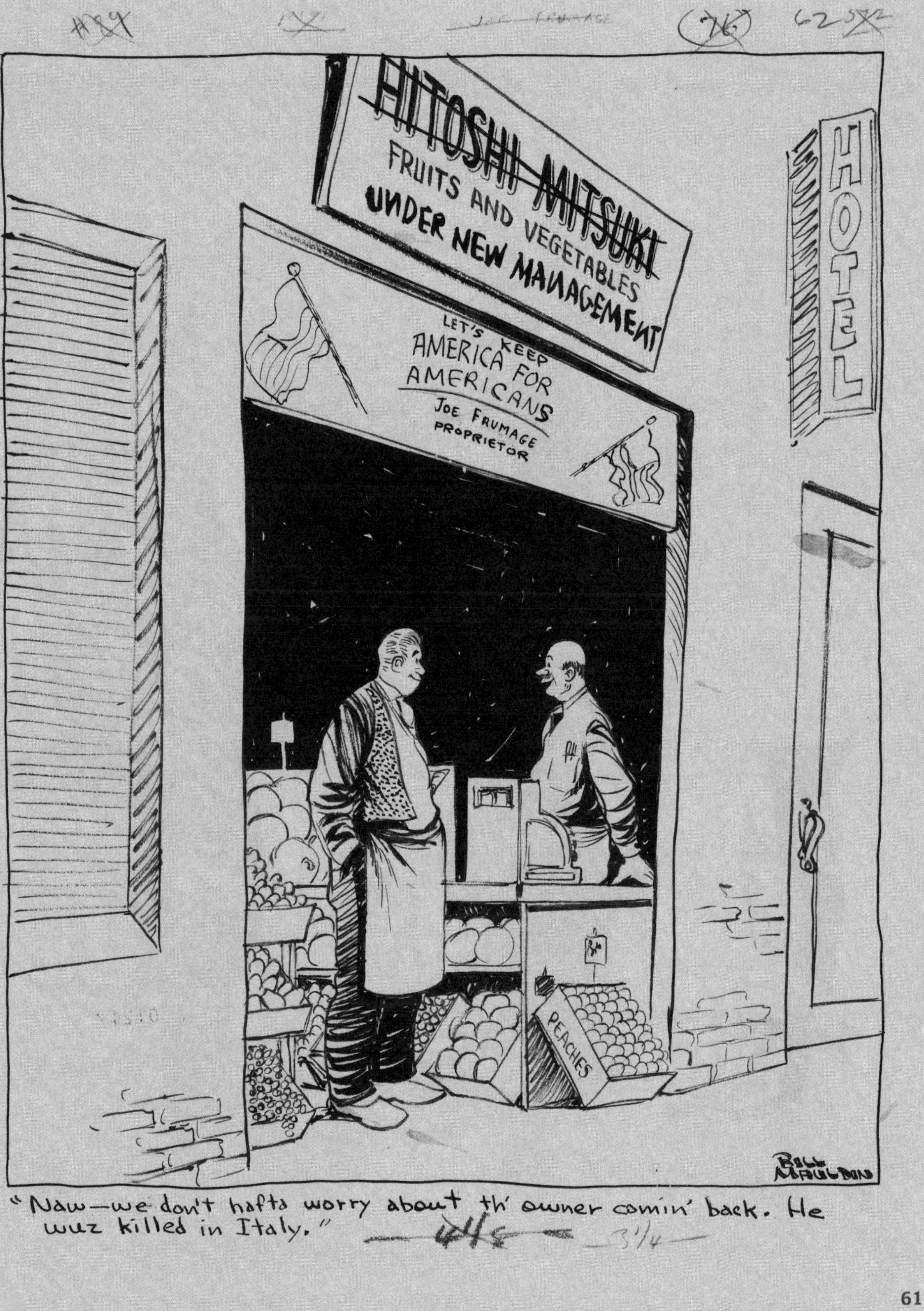
HITOSHI MITSUKI
FRUITS AND VEGETABLES
UNDER NEW MANAGEMENT
LET'S KEEP AMERICA FOR AMERICANS
JOE FRUMAGE PROPRIETOR
HOTEL
PEACHES
BILL MAULDIN

"Naw—we don't hafta worry about th' owner comin' back. He wuz killed in Italy."

" Go home, junior. You're making me look silly. "

icans in the South, while they themselves sat in expensive cafés in Manhattan that lacked any black customers. Mauldin also acknowledged that it took no great courage for him to attack the Klan from his comfortable berth in New York, where a late-night visit from white-sheeted hoodlums was unlikely.

Mauldin also recognized the extent of anti-Semitism present at home and abroad, noting the irony of the United States fighting to overturn Nazi racial doctrines with a Jim Crow army. Looking abroad, he lambasted the British for using German prisoners of war on the Mediterranean island of Cyprus to build a barbed-wire enclosure to hold Jews seeking to reach freedom in Palestine. At the same time, Mauldin regretted both the degree to which the Palestinian question divided Jews and the harsh rhetoric hurled by Zionists and anti-Zionists in support of their positions. In his view, the harsh language provided comfort to anti-Semites and racists.

Mauldin embraced the vision of an America that continued to welcome immigrants who would enrich the fabric of the nation. He supported Secretary of State George Marshall's call for allowing greater numbers

"GO HOME, JUNIOR. YOU'RE MAKING ME LOOK SILLY."
Racial violence remained endemic after V-J Day, with a number of black veterans enduring violence from white racists who wanted to ensure the war did not overturn the racial order. In one particularly grievous case, a black veteran was blinded by a sheriff in South Carolina. (Originally published by United Feature Syndicate, Inc., 1946.)

of Displaced Persons to enter the United States by portraying the retired general relighting the flame atop the Statue of Liberty. Espousing the ethnic pluralism promoted by Franklin D. Roosevelt, he echoed the late president's critique of the Daughters of the Revolution for their overly conservative interpretation of the American past. In Mauldin's estimation, the patriots of '76 look much like Willie and Joe, and if their ghosts came to life, they would cause their DAR ancestors to faint at their sight.

Mauldin saw himself as a mostly liberal independent. He had little tolerance for conservatives who wanted to turn back the clock to Jim Crow and pre–New Deal protections. But he also distanced himself from party-line Communists, even when he found common cause with them on civil rights and other issues. Mauldin's cartoons lamented deteriorating relations between the Soviet Union and the United States. He criticized the Soviet's abridgment of individual liberties and their hypocrisy on the issue of class consciousness. He expressed dismay that the Soviets were writing out the roles of the United States and Great Britain in World War II in their national memory. He found it hypocritical that the Soviet Union, ostensibly a government representing the proletariat, would allow their United Nations ambassador to live in one of the poshest neighborhoods in Manhattan.

Mauldin had no illusions that Soviet leader Joseph Stalin and his regime were Jeffersonian Democrats, and he was critical of their suppressing dissent. At the same time, Mauldin was reluctant to embrace a binary view of the world that saw the Soviet Union as an intractable enemy. Although not naive about the nature of the Soviet system, he had clear misgivings about quickly turning a former ally into an enemy. He defended former Communists who fought against fascism during the Spanish Civil War and World War II. Those seeking to rehabilitate Franco's Spain and Peron's Argentina and to hastily reconcile with Germany earned Mauldin rebukes in several hard-edged cartoons. In one, Mauldin asks how executing prisoners by firing squad upholds the supposed Christian principles of Franco's regime.

In *Back Home*, the lines of the Cold War had not been fully drawn, but many signs pointed to a growing ideological divide between the Soviet Union and the West. The year 1947 represented a critical period in the worsening of relations with the Soviet Union. President Harry S. Truman sought appropriations from Congress to support the Greek and Turkish governments. He argued that the United States must aid these regimes in order to stop the spread of totalitarianism. Fear of internal subversion affected a growing number of self-appointed vigilantes in Congress and the press, and also in the Truman administration, which imposed loyalty tests on federal employees. Mauldin satirized the pervasive surveillance of suspected subversives. But, he also dismissed

ex–American Communists who issued public repentances for their political errors in order to peddle their autobiographies.

At the same time, Mauldin's writing in 1947 failed to fully anticipate the rapid changes that would come to America's relations with the world. A year later, Secretary of State George Marshall announced his program to rebuild Europe at a conference that would initially be attended by the Soviet Union and other Eastern bloc nations. The decision of the Soviet Union and their allies to abandon the conference and spurn offers of aid through the Marshall Plan represented another sign of worsening East-West tensions. In the same year, the State of Israel declared independence and received diplomatic recognition from the United States, and the internecine divisions over a Jewish state began to recede among American Jews. The formation of the North Atlantic Treaty Organization (NATO) came in 1949. This mutual defense pact bound the United States to defend Western Europe in the event of an invasion from the Soviet Union or other hostile nations.

FREEDOM'S BRAVE SENTINELS
Although focusing on the actions of private vigilantes, Mauldin's cartoon could also be read as a critique of the FBI and other government agencies' surveillance of suspect subversives. Mauldin himself came under FBI surveillance for his alleged subversive activities. (Originally published by United Feature Syndicate, Inc., 1947.)

Freedom's brave sentinels

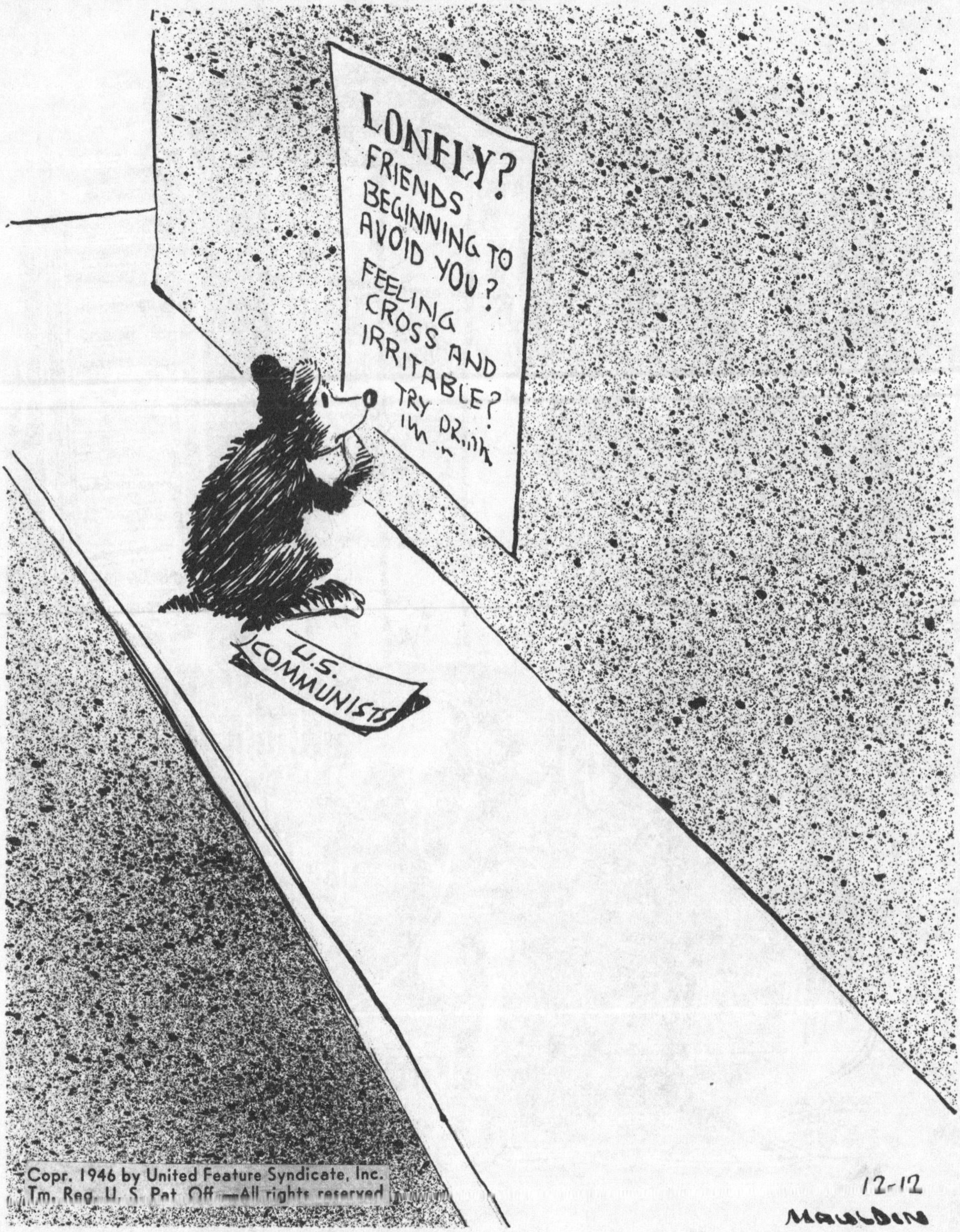
LONELY?
FRIENDS BEGINNING TO AVOID YOU?
FEELING CROSS AND IRRITABLE?
TRY
U.S. COMMUNISTS
Copr. 1946 by United Feature Syndicate, Inc.
Tm. Reg. U. S. Pat. Off.—All rights reserved
12-12
MAULDIN

Although pessimistic about the international outlook, especially the ability of the United Nations to forestall future wars, Mauldin did not abandon hope or embrace cynicism. His experiences as a soldier made him a realist on one important count: he embraced Universal Military Training and lent his name to support Truman's plan to make it a mandate of citizenship for all men. In this instance, Mauldin ran up against significant popular opposition, especially among religious leaders, who feared the militarization of America's youth.

One of the most consistent themes in Mauldin's cartoons is his defense of the First Amendment. Mauldin spoke proudly of his membership in the American Civil Liberties Union. He applauded the principled stand of the organization to defend not only the rights of Communists to appear on the ballot of a Midwestern state, but also of the right of the ultra conservative demagogue Gerald L. K. Smith to speak in a municipal auditorium.

U.S. COMMUNISTS

Even during the Great Depression of the 1930s and later during World War II with the Soviet Union as an ally, membership in the American Communist Party remained small. Party members did have a small following in Hollywood, among civil rights activists, and organized labor. Mauldin clearly took aim at those who overreacted and saw the Communist Party in the United States as grave threat to American society. (Originally published by United Feature Syndicate, Inc., 1946.)

There is much Mauldin was silent about in *Back Home,* including labor strife, women's rights, and partisan politics. Mauldin also said little about the psychological toll the war had on GIs. Though recounting the difficulties of adjusting to civilian life, Mauldin makes only passing mention of the emotional scars of war. Mauldin took strong issue with the popular impression that the war had broken a whole generation of men, turning them into potentially violent criminals. He was much more willing to acknowledge the physical scars of war, depicting veterans in wheelchairs or walking with crutches.

The final and most complex issue Mauldin addressed in *Back Home* was how market pressures shaped the media, including his syndicated features. While some conservative papers dropped his cartoons for ideological reasons, United Feature Syndicate started censoring his work, not because of its ideology, but rather its failure to please a mass audience. Mauldin argued that those on the left needed to create good copy that would appeal to readers. He noted the Hearst chain carried Walter Winchell's columns due to their popularity, even though the columnist's opinions certainly remained opposed to those found in the rest of the chain's newspapers. In his own case, ideological considerations played a role in the New York *World-Telegram* dropping his cartoons, because in the view of the publisher, Mauldin seemed to be following the Communist party line. To his great satisfac-

"There's a small item on page 17 about a triple-axe murder. ~~The killer was a 4-F.~~ ~~veterans involved."~~

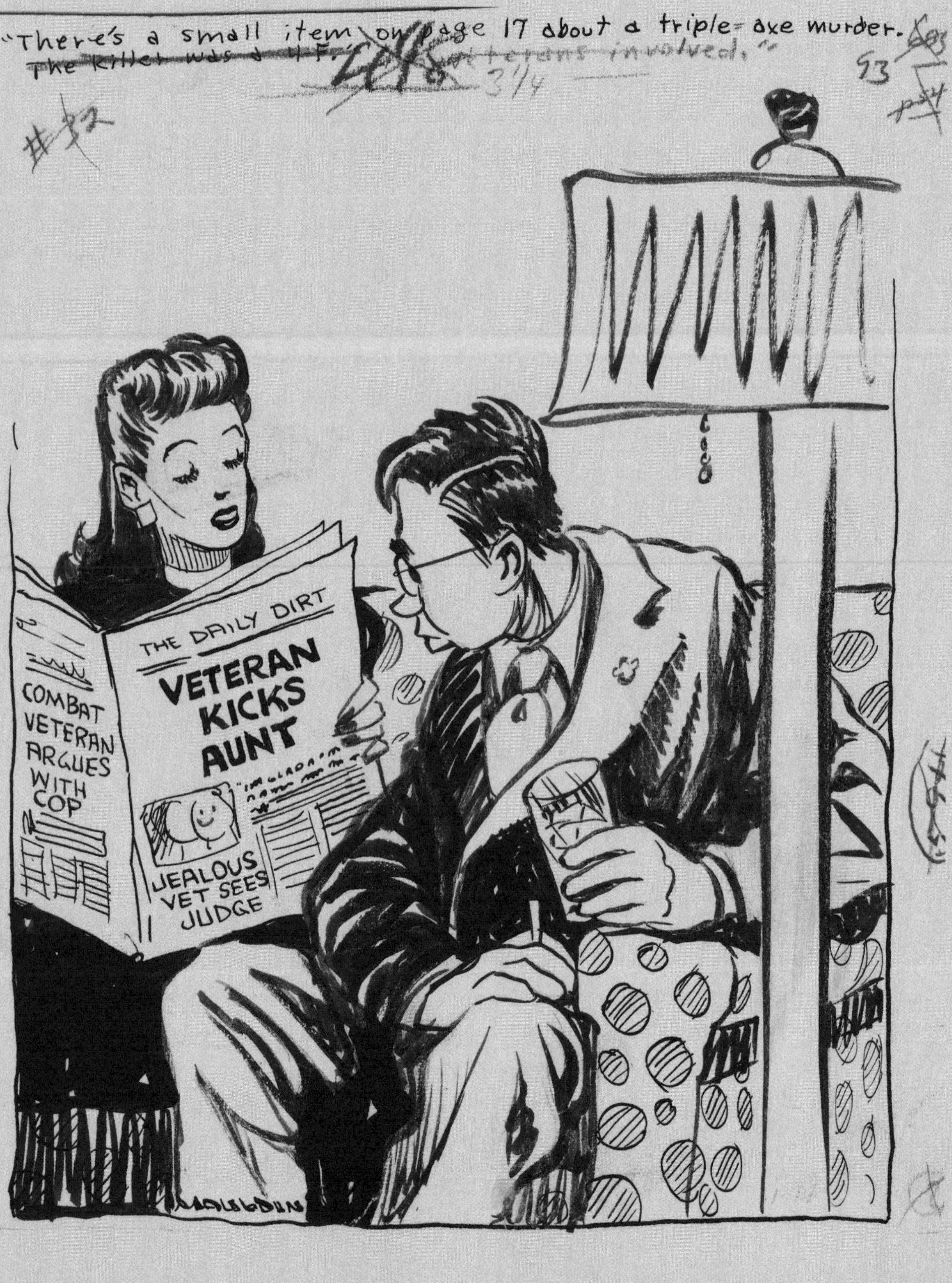
THE DAILY DIRT
VETERAN KICKS AUNT
COMBAT VETERAN ARGUES WITH COP
JEALOUS VET SEES JUDGE

tion, the *New York Herald Tribune* picked up his cartoons and published every one, even when they clashed with the editorial position of the paper.

Mauldin chafed at the pressures of working for a syndicate and would have welcomed working for only one newspaper. He found pleasing dozens of editors at the same time a nearly impossible task, but he also recognized that the economics of the business demanded syndication because it was cheaper. Mauldin reminded us that even in one of the golden ages of print journalism, financial pressures still constrained journalists and editorial cartoonists.

In sum, Mauldin conveyed an air of optimism in *Back Home* while still acknowledging the myriad problems besetting the country. He offered a sense that American veterans, if given access to housing and decent jobs, would be able to readjust to civilian life and that the nation as a whole might emerge from the greatest war in history a wiser, more tolerant, and more generous power. In so doing, he found success in making the transition from soldier to civilian.

"THERE'S A SMALL ITEM ON PAGE 17 ABOUT A TRIPLE AXE MURDER".
Many civilians feared that combat veterans who were psychologically scarred by the war would engage in violence once they returned home. Mauldin satirized the perspective that veterans have a propensity for engaging in violent crimes. (Originally published by United Feature Syndicate, Inc., 1947.)

BILL MAULDIN GOES TO KOREA
→CORD A. SCOTT

On June 25, 1950, Communist North Korea (the Democratic People's Republic of Korea, or DPRK) shocked the world by invading its U.S.-allied neighbor to the south, the Republic of Korea. Two days later, the Truman administration mobilized U.S. forces to assist South Korea. Less than five years after the end of World War II, the nation was embroiled in another war. The fighting would seesaw and then grind along the 38th Parallel, dividing the two countries until the uneasy cease fire of July 27, 1953.

The idea of sending Bill Mauldin to Korea to cover this new conflict was inevitable and so irresistible to publishers that they competed with one another for the honor. *Collier's* won the bidding and hired Mauldin as their illustrator-correspondent in early 1952. The result was a series of essays that would be collected in a book, *Bill Mauldin in Korea*, released later in the year by publisher W. W. Norton.

Mauldin arrived in the war's second year, after the chaotic swings of the first, when the conflict ranged from one end of the peninsula to the other. By 1952, the war had settled into a static confrontation akin to World War I: redoubts, defensive positions, and battles that took place over a small measure of fortified land along the 38th Parallel. The possibility of a cease fire was ever-present, causing occasional combat pauses among soldiers unwilling to get wounded if an armistice was near.

Mauldin took a different approach in Korea than he had years before in Italy and France. As with his previous book, *A Sort of a Saga*, about his childhood, he began with a written narrative and used his artwork to augment it, rather than build the prose around the art. For Korea, Mauldin set the narrative in the form of correspondence between Willie and Joe, profiling the war there against WWII's Italian campaign. Joe, now a war correspondent serving in Korea, narrates most of the book, with Willie providing commentary. As always, the two

EVEN JUST RIDING IN A CAR YOU FEEL LIKE YOU'RE ON ANOTHER PLANET

Mauldin was detained in Japan as he awaited press credentials for travel to Korea. While waiting, he observed life in a country of jarring juxtapositions, the modern and the ancient running up against each other everywhere. (Copyright © 1952 by Bill Mauldin. Courtesy of Bill Mauldin Estate LLC.)

characters reflected Mauldin's own reactions to what he encountered as he empathized with ordinary soldiers.

Mauldin noted the direct similarities between Willie and Joe's time in Italy and the conditions in Korea. Korea was mountainous, with extreme swings in weather conditions. Average GIs knew little about the larger strategy of the war and focused intensely on their immediate environments.

Mauldin also used his transit to Korea through Japan as an opportunity to explore a country and culture not well understood by American readers. Japan was the Korean War's most important staging ground, where key support units and headquarters were located. While in Tokyo, Mauldin captured local color, such as American cars navigating narrow Japanese streets. His writing and illustrations also juxtapose traditional Japanese manners and dress next to the hustle and bustle of westernized life. Even something like a hibachi (a brazier with hot coals used for both cooking and heating) was noted with humor by Mauldin, when Joe burns his feet and socks due to careless proximity to the grill. He himself noted that "everybody writes a book after a trip to the Far East."

As he had done in World War II, Mauldin focused on the privileges of rank and the prevalence of "chickenshit" in Korea. In an ironic twist, Mauldin was given credentials equivalent to a major, much unlike his characters, who were lowly privates and reflex-ively had a distrust of officers.

Mauldin noted serious differences between the structures of U.S. armed forces in World War II and in Korea. In Korea, personnel were not expected to serve in constant battle conditions like WWII, but were placed on a year rotation to maintain better morale. The food was also better in Korea. Mauldin got a broader view of the other branches of service—Marines, Air Force, and Navy especially—and how they related with one another. He never had that perspective during WWII.

Some of Joe's observations in Korea were almost precisely the same as in Italy years earlier. Mauldin didn't feel the need to be in the thick of the fighting, but he also didn't want simply to stay out of harm's way in a headquarters position. Joe discusses "garritroopers"—rear-echelon military—as he awaits transport to the frontlines. He notes that the rearguard troops are generally morose, as the support troops could not earn the points needed to return to the States. In terms of the fighting itself, details in the artwork were reminiscent of Mauldin's WWII work: bitter cold, never-ending patrols with all the associated visions of debris, and the

THEY SAID THEY WERE THINKING ABOUT SURRENDERING Although racial caricature predominated American imagery of Korean allies and enemies during the war, Mauldin eschewed cartoon stereotypes and sought a measure of realism in his depictions of combatants. (Copyright © 1952 by Bill Mauldin. Courtesy of Bill Mauldin Estate LLC.)

omnipresent fear of harm. Mauldin noted that early on, war correspondents were so numerous they could have been armed and thrown into battle, and some were. Mauldin wrote that the artillery and air power of the North Koreans and Chinese were not nearly as deadly or as consistent as the German attacks in Italy. His descriptions were also reflective of the changes in the Army. The troops were now racially integrated, which was the great "social experiment" that Truman instituted. Mauldin welcomed the change.

For those in combat, the monotony could become a story in itself, and Mauldin was quick to pick up on the old themes of life at the front, with illustrations that were both humorous and poignant. They captured the biting winds and snow and the vicious fighting of Korea in January, as well as the quilted uniforms and sneakers of the Chinese People Volunteers (CPV) Army, the distinctive charcoal braziers used by the troops in the field to stay warm, and the ubiquitous A-frame carriers favored by Korean laborers and soldiers to carry loads to the front.

The one aspect that distinguishes Mauldin's work on Korea from the illustrations of other cartoonists is that his are consistently realistic even if they do not appear as fin-

HIS FACE WAS SO DIRTY I COULD'VE SWORN IT WAS YOU FOR A MINUTE, WILLIE

← Mauldin sketched this image at an outpost on the front line. Joe wrote to Willie, "For a second I thought he was you!" (Copyright © 1952 by Bill Mauldin. Courtesy of Bill Mauldin Estate LLC.)

ON SOME COLD NIGHTS A PATROL CAN'T KEEP FROM COUGHING AND SNEEZING

Mauldin captured the extreme combat conditions he encountered along the 38th Parallel in Korea. The weather, he said, was reminiscent of Italy in 1944, except colder. (Copyright © 1952 by Bill Mauldin. Courtesy of Bill Mauldin Estate LLC.) ↓

I SWEAR EVEN THE MUD IS DUSTY
Recalling the footslogging experience of the Italian campaign, Mauldin sketched this Korean War soldier's battle with a ubiquitous enemy: mud. (Copyright © 1952 by Bill Mauldin. Courtesy of Bill Mauldin Estate LLC.)

3 7/16

ished as his other pieces for the book. None of the characters, especially those of enemy combatants, relied on stereotypical cartoon features. His illustrations of the Chinese, North and South Koreans, and Japanese were not done with buckteeth, large glasses, or any of the other tropes common in visual media of that time. His drawings were life sketches and not caricatures.

Officer humor remained a staple of Mauldin's work in Korea. One chapter was titled "The Education of a Shavetail" and depicted how a new lieutenant adjusted from the theoretical aspect of combat to the reality in the field. The descriptions were like those of any commander toward a subordinate: take care of the men, and they will take care of you. There was also second-guessing strategic command. Similar to his commentary on Patton in World War II, Mauldin did take a couple of swipes at MacArthur, especially in terms of the underestimation of the Chinese in the fall of 1950 and the detrimental results of that assessment.

On the whole, Mauldin was still holding to his roots of relating the material to the average reader, who was more often an enlisted man than an officer. Topics like hot food, alcohol, and living conditions were fair game for the commentary and are still universal for combatants when those things cannot be obtained during a battle. Willie tells Joe to play nicely with the officers and gain a safe, clean billet well behind the lines at a division HQ.

The images from the front were rich in detail and harkened back to the WWII prints. The prints are often done in earthen tones that reflect the conditions of mud and cold. One particular illustration, which shows a soldier in a fortified position, is directly reminiscent of WWII, and Mauldin captions it as: "His face was so dirty I could've sworn it was you for a minute, Willie." A two-page illustration in the same chapter, which shows soldiers on patrol in firing positions despite being sick, again gives the reader a sense of the cold, damp conditions soldiers encountered while reconnoitering.

Mauldin later spent time with a Marine engineer unit. Much of the eastern part of the Korean peninsula is even more mountainous, and the terrain often played a far more integral part for military engineering for bridges, roads, and fortifications. Joe commented to Willie the trepidation of getting involved with the Marines, reflecting Mauldin's own feelings, but because of their fighting reputation and the necessity of going where a reporter could offer a bit of insight and humor for the audience, he knew it was necessary. One item of wry humor was the oft-noted service theme of "Go places. Join the U.S. Marines" for their way of seeing the world. It was during his time with this unit that Mauldin also discussed another aspect of the war not often shown: war orphans. One particular vignette features the war orphan Chu, who served as an unofficial mascot for the engineer unit. The

NOBODY ON A CARRIER WALKS STANDING STRAIGHT UP

Mauldin circulated among all branches of service during his Korean tour. One stop was aboard an aircraft carrier, where Mauldin was struck by the difficult sea and wind conditions, as well as the new jet aircraft and associated assault tactics. (Copyright © 1952 by Bill Mauldin. Courtesy of Bill Mauldin Estate LLC.)

child had picked up on Marine mannerisms such as calling out pogues ("persons other than grunts:" noncombat marines) as well as the colorful phrases and mannerisms associated with combatants in general and Marines in particular. Mauldin's color print of this meeting is striking, as one has a small child in a red shirt trying to act tough, while he was backed by several large formidable Marines. It was similar to the Warner Broth-

THIS KOREAN KID WAS BACKED UP BY THE BIGGEST, ROUGHEST MARINE SERGEANTS I EVER SAW

Korea was awash in war orphans in 1952. Some were adopted as houseboys by marine units. In return for doing chores, they were provided with food, a warm place to sleep, and perhaps some fun as a mascot. Mauldin captured a Marine Corps mascot on his visit to an engineer unit. (Copyright © 1952 by Bill Mauldin. Courtesy of Bill Mauldin Estate LLC.)

ers cartoon with the small dog who barks loudly but is backed by a large (devil) dog in the background.

Mauldin's next reporting jaunt was with the Navy and its role, which was integral to the war effort. One theme that often ran through not just Mauldin's cartoons, but also those of *Stars and Stripes,* was the recall of WWII veterans to fight in Korea for their specific skill sets. For the Navy, many pilots were recalled to active duty, and Mauldin noted that the pilots looked like old men, even though many were in their thirties at best. He also illustrated some of the images aboard a carrier as it conducted air operations. The winds buffeting the flight crews as they walked on deck, or the new jets flying above the carrier were also noted. One can feel the elements of the sea through the artwork.

Mauldin couldn't help but color his reporting with a story of Joe pulling strings aboard ship to get a shower and several examples of the better living conditions Navy personnel experienced as opposed to their Army counterparts in foxholes. Willie later responded to Joe by commenting on the "chickenshit" nature of naval officers and the threat they both had faced when they crossed into "officer's country" while aboard a troopship in the Mediterranean in World War II.

The last chapter of the book focuses on the treaty negotiations at the Panmunjom site, just north of the original 38th Parallel. The illustrations centered on the pomp of the negotiations as well as the various observations made by people near the tents where the talks were held. One of the most interesting and insightful of the illustrations was the one in which the North Korean delegate is dressed in a haughty manner, complete with a cigarette holder and outlandish shoulder boards for his uniform coat, while his Chinese counterpart looks on in amusement wearing his "people's" outfit with no signifiers of rank. The illustration from the book offers a good perception of the pomp involved in the negotiations, but the original color work highlights it even more, displaying the bright uniforms of the North Korean officers, who seem almost toylike, while the Chinese delegate's drab garb reveals this negotiator to represent the working elements of the war as well as the talks. This pomposity was in direct contrast to the fighting by 1952, in which the Chinese were the principal combatants on the communist side, while the North Korean army was reduced in size and importance. Mauldin was so shocked by the North Korean mannerisms, the jokes and swipes he often took at the pomposity of U.S. officers seemed less humorous by comparison.

Mauldin joked that the Soviet vehicles driven by the North Koreans and Chinese to the site were long on image and short on practicality. He also drew a sympathetic scene of two North Korean soldiers "goldbricking" by lounging and smoking rather than patrolling. In this regard they were

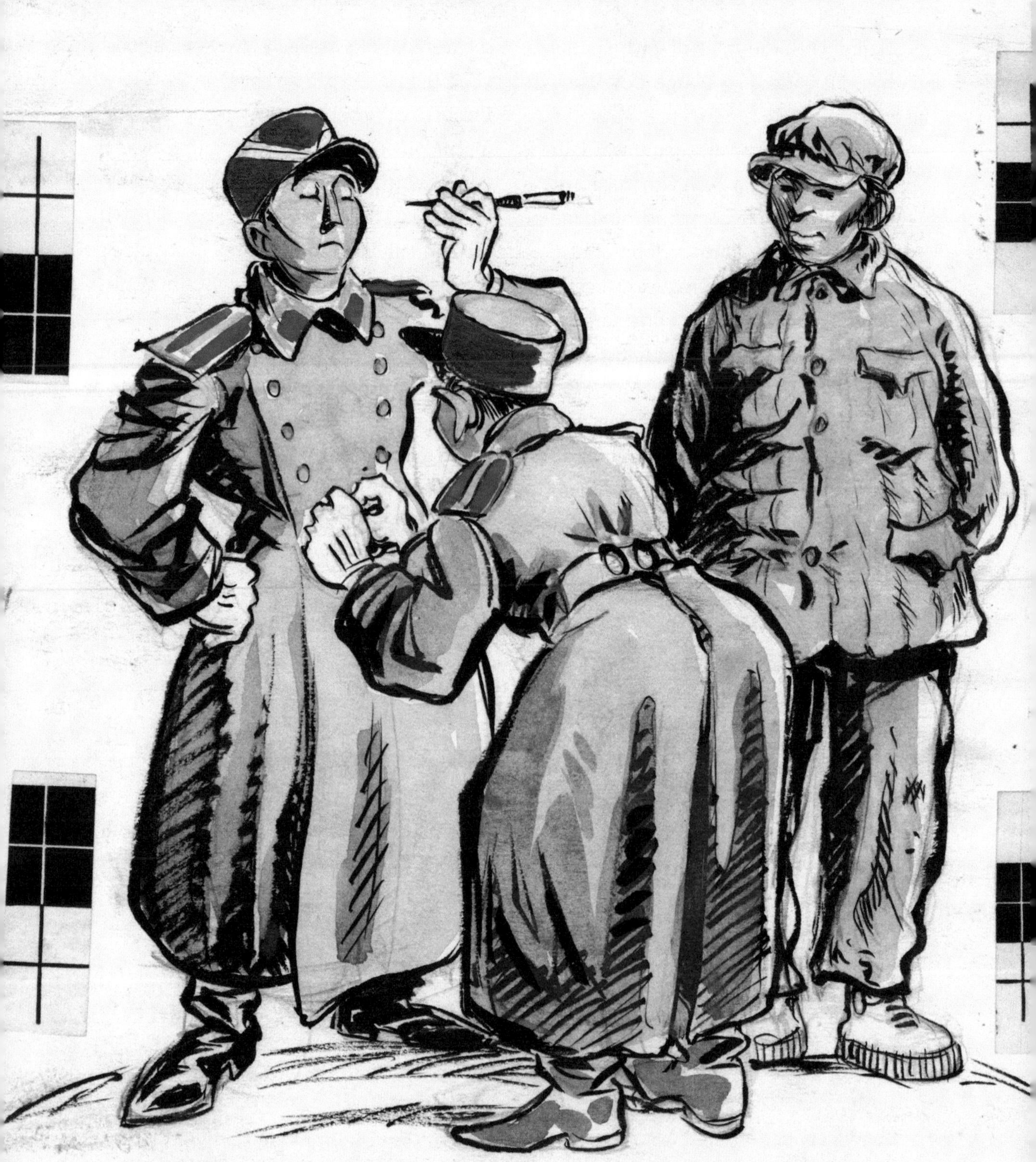

acting exactly as Willie and Joe might have if the situation were in a different setting. Mauldin, in the actual situation, wanted to make contact with the goldbrickers but was advised against it.

The overall illustrations for the book vary at times in regard to style, color tone, and detail, as befitting the subjects. The battle scenes are done with the heaviness of the conditions, akin to the seriousness of combat in Korea.

Bill Mauldin in Korea doesn't offer a lot of insight into the rationale of the war, but rather, in Mauldin's patented style, gives readers an idea of the sacrifices and conditions in which ordinary people serve. It presents the unique perspective of a famous WWII enlisted veteran on a different, more complicated conflict. While *Bill Mauldin in Korea* produces the visual punch of his World War

II work, it's not as voluminous. The book is also a reflection of how Mauldin as a person was evolving in his worldview, relaying those views not through his own thoughts so much, but through his characters.

Mauldin's war cartoons from Korea would pave the way for later commentary on the Vietnam war and even served as the basis for a book on the experiences of the Revolutionary War soldier, which was produced around the time of the U.S. bicentennial (*Mud and Guts*, 1978). These books are humorous, depict commonalities of soldiers regardless of era, and often serve as a springboard for further historical discussion, as the author has done in U.S. history survey classes. Mauldin's reporting and insight have endured and inspired journalists and illustrators to the present day.

THE COCKY LITTLE NORTH KOREANS KIND OF AMUSE THE CHINESE

Mauldin spotted a scene that defied caricature outside the negotiating tents at Panmunjom. A North Korean martinet in showy dress with "shoulder boards as big as shingles" is tended to obsessively by a minion while a Chinese delegate looks on in bemusement. The scene dampened Mauldin's enthusiasm for criticizing the inequities in the U.S. military. (Copyright © 1952 by Bill Mauldin. Courtesy of Bill Mauldin Estate LLC.)

KOREAN WAR CARTOONISTS

CORD A. SCOTT

Bill Mauldin's Willie and Joe cast a long shadow over the work of other military cartoonists during the Korean War. As in World War II, *Stars and Stripes* and other news outlets mobilized comic artists for Korea to boost the morale of American GIs. Many of them imitated Mauldin.

In 1951, Bill Hume was stationed at the Naval Air Station at Yokosuka, Japan, when he created *Babysan* for the station newspaper. The feature focused on the mix-ups and confusions of American servicemen relating to Japanese girls and culture. With John Annarino helping write the dialogue, *Babysan* became a hit and inspired Hume to create a series of comic books to reach a wider GI audience, starting with *Babysan: A Private Look at the Japanese Occupation* (1953).

This anonymous submission to *Stars and Stripes* during the Korean War plays off (or steals from) Mauldin's WWII cartoon about a beautiful town in the Alps being "either the enemy or off limits." As in WWII, GIs in Korea found that as soon as a town was liberated, MPs would immediately place it off-limits. (Copyright © 1952, 2020 *Stars and Stripes.* All Rights Reserved.)

EUSAK 'n Jon

TROELSTRUP

"Don't rightly know, sarge . . . c'mon in, s'down, and I'll see if he's here!"

During the war, *Stars and Stripes* also published hundreds of cartoons submitted by anonymous GIs. One such cartoon appeared in 1952 in Mauldin's patented strong, dark style. It shows a baby-faced MP placing a town off-limits even while the fighting still rages all around it.

Several other cartoons echoed Mauldin's focus on the weather's effect on morale and fighting posture. A cartoon attributed to Glenn Troelstrup, titled "EUSAK 'n Jon,"

shows two Willie and Joe–type characters, one who is in a far-too-small tent, while the other stands over him, both in the rain.

Marine Norval Packwood, author of *Leatherhead in Korea* (1952), also emulated Mauldin's style of artistic storytelling. More cartoonlike than Mauldin's work, *Leatherhead in Korea* sought to capture the basic frustrations of the average grunt. Packwood had served in combat and used anecdotes from that experience as cartoon punch lines. Packwood was brought up with the concept that "every Marine is a rifleman" and should be ready to fight, even if serving in a support unit. But his work circulated mainly among Marines and didn't have the exposure that Mauldin had with *Stars and Stripes* in World War II.

"*The major says this patrol don't have to fight, or even take a prisoner. All ya gotta do is to see how much fire ya can draw.*"

"THE MAJOR SAYS THIS PATROL DON'T HAVE TO FIGHT, OR EVEN TAKE A PRISONER. ALL YOU GOTTA DO IS SEE HOW MUCH FIRE YOU CAN DRAW."

This cartoon by staff artist Al Summer appeared in the *45th Division News* during the Korean War. Its gallows humor owes much to the newspaper's first cartoonist, Bill Mauldin. Summers didn't copy Mauldin's style or level of detail but rather used his sardonic approach as a template. (Copyright © 1952, 2020 *Stars and Stripes.* All Rights Reserved.)

"DON'T TAKE MY PICTURE—I'M A CORRESPONDENT! THERE'S A COMBAT MAN OVER THERE!"

Perhaps the best military cartoonist of the Korean War was Staff Sergeant Norval E. Packwood Jr., who served in Korea from 1951 to 1952 as a combat artist for the *Marine Corps Gazette.* Packwood's humor was in the vein of Mauldin's, though his style was more in the "big foot" school of cartooning. On this page, Packwood expresses a Marine rifleman's jaundiced view of airmen and correspondents. (Originally published in *Leatherhead in Korea,* 1952. Courtesy of Gene Packwood.)

"Ah cain't agree you Irish woulda lost this
war without allies like Texas an' Russia."

BILL MAULDIN'S LEGACY IN MILITARY CARTOONING←
CHRISTINA M. KNOPF

Wise beyond his years, Linus looks out from the news page and tells readers that "Bill Mauldin was the most famous cartoonist to come out of World War II."

Snoopy agrees, adding, "He drew great mud."

This *Peanuts* strip was one of many Veterans Day tributes that cartoonist and World War II veteran Charles Schulz made to his idol Bill Mauldin. Snoopy, as WWI Flying Ace or wearing an Ike jacket, would head to Mauldin's to "quaff a few root beers" with "ol' Bill." Snoopy's bird friends also got in on the act, donning combat helmets and declaring themselves to be Willie and Joe—Mauldin's iconic GI characters. Once, in 1998, Snoopy even joined Mauldin's dogface soldiers at the muddy front in a strip co-created by Schulz and Mauldin, the only time another artist's work appeared in *Peanuts*. Schulz acknowledged Mauldin as a friend and hero and made occasional allusions to his work. One of the Veterans Day tributes featured Linus telling Snoopy that he always liked the cartoon where a captain looks out at a sunset and says, "Beautiful view! Is there one for the enlisted men?" In a *Peanuts* strip about summer camp, Linus complains about the rain and quips, quoting Willie, "This tree leaks."

Bill Mauldin's legacy lives on in the work of other cartoonists, particularly those in the military.

"AH CAIN'T AGREE. YOU IRISH WOULDA LOST THIS WAR WITHOUT ALLIES LIKE TEXAS AN' RUSSIA."
Café scenes such as this one, with Bill Mauldin's Willie and Joe in 1944, were re-created by Charles Schulz when Snoopy as a WWII Veteran or a WWI Flying Ace would quaff root beer in honor of past wars. (Originally published by *Stars and Stripes,* 1944.)

"In case you're captured you can eat the message...I had it printed on rolled pizza!..."

⬆ MAP STRATEGY

Bill Mauldin's work was known for capturing the absurdities of military hierarchy and regulations. Vernon E. Grant's cartoons from the Vietnam War, such as this one, often did likewise. (Courtesy of Bvgrant Studios, 1969.)

Bill Mauldin's favorite Mauldin cartoon was of a tough old cavalry sergeant putting a broken jeep out of its misery. He drew several versions of its throughout his career. Here, Steve Opet quotes the famed cartoon to lampoon warfare's newest and often frustrating technology. (Courtesy of 10th Mountain Division & Fort Drum Museum, 2008.) ➡

FIGHTING CARTOONISTS

Mauldin was, as *Business Insider* once said, "the WWII veteran [who] inspired almost every comic strip." As the most famous "fighting cartoonist," Mauldin focused on both the comedic elements of combat (its uncertainty, absurdity, and dissonance) and the ironic humorlessness of the military structure (its hierarchy, bureaucracy, and rigidity). "Miltoons," like Mauldin's especially, offer enlisted men and women something to laugh at even when life is not that funny. Military humor helps to strengthen community, buoy morale, teach valuable—even life-saving—lessons, make sense of war, and express universal concerns about daily life.

Soldiers have drawn cartoons to record their lot in life since at least the Napoleonic Wars. Since then, certain themes repeat themselves: gripes about food and medical care, peculiarities of foreign populations, the bonds between combat soldiers, the joyless celebration of survival, and a tempered animosity for officers and regulations. Military cartoons also rely on more common gags not specific to the military. Some, such as Mauldin's, engage comedic social commentary—humor shaped by the experience of combat. These cartoons are reflective and raw. They are not laugh-out-loud funny, but instead provoke a knowing smile of shared misery or a wry chuckle at a lived truth.

The American Civil War was replete with "off-hand" amputation puns. Doughboy humor helped recruits of World War I to adapt to military life by suggesting the universality of their experiences and challenges. Humor was a key part of the total mobilization of men, women, and children in World War II, comforting, motivating, commemorating. Military cartooning continued through the war in Korea, supported by military morale officers as a means of helping soldiers cope with life in a foreign country and the regimentation of military service. In Vietnam, underground publications expanded the universe of military cartoons. Mauldin continued to work through it all, making visual observations about war and politics as an editorial cartoonist.

MODERN MAULDINS

Mauldin's work is the gold standard for latter-day cartoonists. Vernon E. Grant, whose cartoons of the war in Vietnam were featured in *Stars and Stripes* under the title *Grant's Grunts,* John Holmes's *Power Point Ranger*, and Mark Baker's *Pvt. Murphy's Law* all, like Mauldin's, offer the grunt's perspective on military life.

W. C. Pope, creator of *Pope's Puns,* the official cartoon of the Air Force Reserve since 1991, was dubbed "the Bill Mauldin of the Air Force" by *Military.com.* During Operation Iraqi Freedom, 10th Mountain Division reservist Steve Opet created a series of cartoons called *Opet's Odyssey*, penned from Camp Victory in Baghdad. The vignettes captured the humor of war's hardships and hierarchies and earned Opet the moniker of "the Bill Mauldin of Iraq." Opet even echoed one of Mauldin's most famous images when he drew a sergeant shooting a computer that read "access denied." CF "Arik" Grant's cartoons of the Iraq War similarly prompted *Stars and Stripes* to compare Grant's *BOHICA Blues* to Mauldin's *Up Front* in its attempt to "humorously capture the feelings, desires, and daily routine of soldiers." Like Opet, Grant paid homage to Mauldin with a 2016 strip in which he replaced two of his regular charac-

ters with images of Willie and Joe. *Publishers Weekly* proclaimed that Maximilian Uriarte, author of the satirical Marine Corps comic strip *Terminal Lance* and the *New York Times* best-selling war graphic novel *The White*

Mauldin often featured interactions between battle-fatigued soldiers and fresh-faced replacements in his cartoons. Here, CF "Arik" Grant uses Mauldin's Willie and Joe as stand-ins for his regular *BOHICA Blues* characters to similarly illustrate the premature aging of soldiers in war. (Courtesy of CF "Arik" Grant, 2016.)

Donkey, is "poised to become a Bill Mauldin for the social media generation."

In terms of style, the new generation of cartoonists have little in common with Mauldin. Mauldin's work is gritty—as Snoopy noted, "he drew great mud." Done in black and white, with pen on paper, his artwork is heavy with lots of textures, shadows, and shading. The style is largely realistic with subtle exaggeration and simplification, such as the basic dots that make his characters' eyes. The newer miltoon creators use more cartoonish styles—less shading, more exaggeration, softer lines, simpler designs, and often color. Mauldin did not consider himself much of a writer, and his artwork came first. For strips like *Power Point Ranger*, whose title itself is a joke, the art is almost secondary to the story. Drawing on the military's overuse of slide-deck presentations, Holmes creates his cartoon with PowerPoint presentation software, resulting in crude, pixelated images done through a blend of geometrical shapes and free-hand lines with few environmental details.

What these cartoons *do* have in common is their honesty. It is the ability to find the humor in bleak circumstances and to give voice to the common soldier that made Mauldin's work famous and that has earned his successors a place beside his name. Mauldin's main characters—the dirty, unshaven, slouching Willie and Joe—became the archetype of the dogface soldier in American popular perception. If Mauldin was the voice of front line soldiers, Willie and Joe were their face. Many of Mauldin's wartime cartoons focused on the hardships of weather and terrain, particularly as exacerbated by inadequate clothing, insufficient food, and equipment problems, all compounded by the absurdities of military hierarchy and regulations, especially the clueless inexperience of officers.

The "Bill Mauldin of Iraq," Steve Opet, likewise chronicled interactions between officers and enlisted and lampooned the strict rules that shaped daily life for soldiers deployed to Iraq. Grant, too, captures the drudgery and discord inherent in military life, poking fun at anything that created grumbling in the ranks. Baker's Pvt. Murphy was often found griping about Army rules and subsequently getting in trouble with his commanding officers—though he was proud of his fellow grunts. Holmes was purposeful in using politically incorrect humor as a means to call out institutional and institutionalized hypocrisy. Pope captured a love-hate relationship with equipment and technology in the Air Force, as well as the frustrations with the procedures for using them. And though Uriarte had no idea who Bill Mauldin was when he started cartooning his Marine Corps experiences, the "Bill Mauldin for the social media generation" seemingly emulates Mauldin's cartoons in documenting the many small indignities that come with serving in the lower ranks.

▶GRUMBLING IN THE RANKS

Just as Grant, Holmes, Opet, Pope, Uriarte, and others are "the Bill Mauldins" of their wars, Mauldin in World War II was called "the Bairnsfather of this war" by Gen. George Patton. England's Capt. Bruce Bairnsfather was the most famous cartoonist of the Great War. He served on the front with the 1st Battalion, Royal Warwickshire Regiment. His ironic strips demonstrated humor through every possible difficulty and challenge. Like Mauldin after him, Bairnsfather found amusement in what he described in his memoir as war's "absurdity, the stark, fearful predicament." His work appeared throughout trench newspapers of the allied forces and in multiple collected volumes. Bairnsfather's cartoons were about, and relatable to, the common soldier. They typified Allied military humor of World War I in their celebration of the antiheroism of the citizen soldier. Bairnsfather relied heavily on the archetype of the "grumpy Tommy"—bedraggled soldiers, tired, cynical, and all but detached from the horrors around them. Bairnsfather was considered "The Man Who Won the War" for the morale boost his cartoons gave to those at the front lines, and his war-weary characters of Old Bill, Bert, and Alfie inspired the 1926 film *The Better 'Ole*, starring Syd Chaplin, among a number of other dramatic productions.

Three decades later, Mauldin's career followed a similar trajectory. His work was featured in camp publications, the *45th Division News*, and *Stars and Stripes*, before appearing on the home front through United Feature Syndicate. With a subsequent Pulitzer prize, best-selling book, and Hollywood movie deal, Mauldin eclipsed Bairnsfather in both fame and fortune. It is the latter who is now described as "the British 'Bill Mauldin' of World War I."

Both Mauldin and Bairnsfather irritated their superiors. Military officials initially worried that Bairnsfather's sarcasm might slow recruitment efforts. Other expressions of soldier humor in World War I, such as the satirical trench paper *The Wipers Times*, were met with a mixture of disapproval and acceptance in the highest ranks. As noted by author John Ivelaw-Chapman, *The Wipers Times* could not have existed outside of active warfare because of the way it disrupted the stringent division between officers and their men, divisions erased in combat scenarios.

Humor can indeed be used as a means of disrupting authoritarian structures or as a type of resistance. According to *Beetle Bailey* cartoonist Mort Walker, "Army cartoons are

"I GOT A HANGOVER. DOES IT SHOW?"

This cartoon from January 1945 plays on ordinary civilian concerns about self-presentation in public to highlight both Willie and Joe's disheveled and grimy appearance and their dependence on alcohol to cope with the trauma of war. It was precisely this kind of cartoon that rankled the spit-and-polish General Patton. (Originally published by *Stars and Stripes*, 1945.)

"I got a hangover. Does it show?"

often considered subversive." *Beetle Bailey* was banned twice from *Stars and Stripes*: once, in the early 1950s, for its disrespectful portrayal of officers, and again in 1970 when Walker introduced an African American officer, Lt. Jack Flap, to the predominantly white cast. Mark Baker responded to an angry unnamed officer in a 1990s *Pvt. Murphy's Law* cartoon by telling the offended, "Don't read it anymore, *Sir*." W. C. Pope's *The Adventures of Arthur Awax* was challenged by a commanding officer in 1983, prompting Pope to remark in *Above & Beyond*, "The best gauge of a cartoonist's success is by the number of officers he's pissed off."

"AIM BETWEEN TH' EYES, JOE . . . SOMETIMES THEY CHARGE WHEN THEY'RE WOUNDED." ➡
Again, Mauldin plays on common civilian observations, this time from hunting, to point up the class indignities of the life up front, including living with every species of vermin. (Originally published by *Stars and Stripes*, 1944.)

⬇ When Mauldin was stationed at Pine Camp in Upstate New York for training from 1942 to 1943, the region's cold, snowy winters were prominent in his cartoons. Pine Camp eventually became Fort Drum, which is still known for its harsh winters, as demonstrated in this 2013 *Doctrine Man* strip. (Courtesy of Steve Leonard, creator of *Doctrine Man*.)

© 2013 The Further Adventures of Doctrine Man!! | www.facebook.com/doctrineman | www.twitter.com/doctrine_man

"Aim between th' eyes, Joe... Sometimes they charge when they're wounded."

The media and the military often have a contentious relationship. Satire is by nature antiauthority. Mauldin earned the wrath of General Patton for portraying soldiers as unkempt and officers as arrogant. Patton reportedly went to great lengths to track down Mauldin, chastising him for making soldiers look like "god-damn bums." In fact, this aspect of his characters was something that Mauldin emphasized and occasionally remarked on within the cartoons. When encountering shocked locals, Willie observes, "We oughta tell 'em the whole army don't look like us, Joe." Patton attempted to have Mauldin's cartoons banned—an effort that was undermined by Mauldin's fans Generals Dwight Eisenhower and Mark Clark. Mauldin responded to Patton with a cartoon in which Willie and Joe are parked in a jeep beside a sign that proclaims they are entering the Third Army and will face fines for having no: helmet, shave, buttons, tie, shine, and/or shampoo, "By order: Ol' Blood and Guts." Rather than get the fine or, worse, clean up, Joe and Willie decide to take a thousand-mile detour around the camp. (Charles Schulz later pokes fun at this by having Snoopy claim that both he and Bill Mauldin were "very close friends of General Patton").

Seventy years later, the Association of the United States Army compared Mauldin running afoul of Patton to an alleged campaign by senior Army officers to discover the identity of the anonymous creator behind the online comic strip *Doctrine Man*. With its

"GIMME MY CANTEEN BACK, WILLIE. I SEE YA SOAKIN' YERBEARD FULL."
(Originally published in *Stars and Stripes*, 1944.)

stick-figure computer art, *Doctrine Man* was designed in 2008 by former Army officer and senior military strategist Steve Leonard—who was then anonymous—to advance professional discourse on national security issues and to engage military community advocacy. Though *Doctrine Man* was a product of relaxed restrictions on social media to allow for unofficial dialoging and networking to promote morale and enable cohesion, the Defense Department never used the strip in its communications. Despite his best efforts to keep the strip respectful, Leonard maintained his anonymity to protect against retribution for insubordination.

The lesson that the work of Mauldin and the experience of Leonard (who is a self-described fan of Mauldin) demonstrates is that even though cartoon satire can be subversive, it is also a socially acceptable means of dissent. Humor leavens criticism, expressing hard truths in a palatable way. Rumpled uniforms, unshaven faces, and dirty bodies are only funny, or rebellious, if readers recognize and accept military standards for appearance. Mocking officers for indolence may make unflattering commentary on their character or experience, but it also provides a reminder to enlisted personnel that shirking is not acceptable within the

"Gimme my canteen back, Willie. I see ya soakin' yer beard full."

BATAAN - 1942
PREASE— WE SIMPRY OBEYING COMMANDS
GERMANY— 1944
SORRY, FRÄULEIN.. VE MERELY DO AS VE'RE TOLD
CREMATORIUM
SIBERIA— ANY TIME
NO OFFENSE, COMRADES... JUST FOLLOWING MY ORDERS!
Chicago Sun-Times
©1971 MAULDIN

GOOD GUYS AT HEART

group. Mauldin was particularly skilled at creating sympathy for his characters and the men they represented, and thus sympathy for their nonconformity. By enduring hardships with grim determination, Willie and Joe encouraged soldiers on the front to maintain their humanity. And his particular brand of self-disparaging humor, captured in his characters' unenthusiastic dedication to the Army, softened the edges of his political commentary. Mauldin might not have always respected military leadership, but he had a great deal of respect for those on the front lines. As observed in the 50th Anniversary Special of *Stars and Stripes* in 1992, "Bill Mauldin, the Pulitzer prize–winning artist from the *Mediterranean Stars and Stripes* staff, had a knack for spotting the inequities in Army life—and then quickly turning inequity into ink."

As one observer noted, Mauldin's potshots at officers were not only about military warfare but also class warfare. Mauldin was an advocate of equity and equality— themes that became more pronounced in his political postwar work, in which he tackled the poor treatment of returning sol-

"GOOD GUYS AT HEART"

Mauldin reflects the new hindsight of history. The cartoon compares the Bataan Death March of 1942, the Nazi crematoriums of 1944, and the Soviet Union's Gulag, each featuring soldiers justifying their crimes by saying they were just following orders. (Originally published by the *Chicago Sun-Times*, 1971.)

diers and a variety of racial, economic, and social concerns that the war had brought to the fore. He was a champion of the downtrodden and often emphasized privation, sacrifice, and suffering. Mauldin's war cartoons featured Willie and Joe living with rats, sharing a single pair of good socks or the last drops of water in a canteen, eating a C-ration as a Christmas feast, using matches to heat coffee, and bathing in mud.

➡ THE REALITY OF WAR STORIES

Unlike their predecessors, Mauldin's cartoons existed in tandem with the assorted depictions of war in popular comic books of the 1940s. Mauldin created Willie and Joe for the *45th Division News* in 1940, the same year that Dell Comics launched *War Stories*, the first comic book dedicated specifically to stories of war. The early war comics were mostly jingoistic stories of action and heroism. They frequently emphasized individualism, depicting the combat experience of a single soldier and his buddy, squad, or platoon—often specialized teams who possessed remarkable, experimental war technology. Heroics, teamwork, obedience, and sacrifice were common themes. Battles were an especially popular focus of attention, usually waged around overly simplified conflicts of good and bad. Moral platitudes and idealized patriotism legitimized violence as an expression of valiant masculinity.

Within this milieu of popular media,

STAR SPANGLED BANTER

BILL MAULDIN

GRENADES

Block out words "Star Spangled Banter" and "Bill Mauldin" so they will be in white without any halftone dots.

Mauldin drew this cover for *Star Spangled Banter*, his first book, during the Louisiana Maneuvers of 1941, before going overseas. His work always improved in kinetic environments, and his comic appreciation for the dangers of war can be glimpsed in this early self-portrait. (Originally published by Universal Press, San Antonio, Texas, 1941.)

Mauldin's work was groundbreaking. In his war comics, soldiers rarely discharged their weapons, and provisions were so inadequate even water was scarce. Even when the newest military technology was available, it could prove to be deadly—as in a poignant cartoon wherein Willie and Joe walk along a road littered with canvas field bags, noting, "I see Comp'ny E got th' new style gas masks." Life debts were repaid in dry socks. And the reality of combat was less about making a glorious charge and more about leaving the safety of a foxhole to urinate.

Mauldin said that infantry soldiers live with so few possessions, only the essentials, that everything they have becomes precious and nothing is taken for granted. While other war comics of the period valorized outsize action and the gung-ho spirit of our fighting men, Mauldin focused on the quotidian aspects of front line life.

Mauldin's cartoons avoided graphic depictions of death, but they did not shy away from violence or its effects. Danger is almost always present, as in a cover illustration for Mauldin's *Star Spangled Banter* that depicts a soldier drawing at a makeshift desk, seated upon a box of grenades while bullets bounce off his combat helmet and artillery shells fly past his head. The presence of artillery and gunfire naturally included, especially for those who experienced it, the suggestion of bodies nearby. The haggard and old-before-their-time appearance of Mauldin's experienced combat soldiers likewise captured the physical and mental ravages of war. Indeed, the premature aging of young men was far more ignominious than the glorious heroism of death in combat. Dark in humor, Mauldin's cartoons emphasized the grim reality of war.

By rejecting the mythic soldier of war propaganda, found in posters and comic books and movies, and promoting the image of the unextraordinary citizen soldier, Mauldin helped to lead the way in fashioning a more compassionate and authentic war genre. Though other voices of World War II more directly shaped the genre—Sam Glanzman, Will Eisner, Jack Kirby, and Stan Lee—they did so in ways consistent with Mauldin's approach to military cartoons, with attention to the small details of daily life, such as bad food, out-of-touch bureaucracy, inadequate or impractical clothing, rotten weather, and the use of slang and jargon. Following the peace and counterculture movements of the 1960s, war comics at large more explicitly included antiwar sentiments and stories that explored the chaos of combat, the futility of war, and the hypocrisy of politics.

Like the famed war reporter Ernie Pyle,

Mauldin served as a correspondent for and of the soldiers. His work should be understood as an early example of graphic reportage or comics journalism—the use of sequential art storytelling to report on, and contextualize, current events. Though comics journalism did not establish itself as a distinct genre until the mid-1990s and was not mainstreamed until the 2010s, it is now renowned for its war coverage, particularly through the work of writer and artist Joe Sacco, whose work includes *Palestine* (1993), *Safe Area Goražde* (2000), *The Fixer: A Story from Sarajevo* (2003), *War's End: Profiles from Bosnia, 1995–96* (2005), and *Footnotes in Gaza* (2009). Sacco is known for the subjectivity of his work, for drawing himself into his stories to acknowledge how his experiences shape his understanding of events. But Mauldin did this first. For example, in 1943, Mauldin was struck by shrapnel from a German mortar, resulting in a minor shoulder wound. A soldier behind him was killed. For his injury, Mauldin received a Purple Heart, despite his protests that he had been hurt worse "sneaking through barbed-wire fences in New Mexico." In 1944, Mauldin's reaction to his decoration is reflected in a cartoon where an injured Willie tells a medic, "Just gimme a couple aspirin. I already got a Purple Heart."

TAPS

There's a timelessness to Mauldin's work, as attested by the appearance of Willie and Joe on the cover of the December 20, 1999, edition of *Newsweek* beneath the words "People of the Century." The lasting legacy of Bill Mauldin was apparent upon his death in 2003 when dozens of cartoonists visually paid their respects through their craft, emulating the late, great Mauldin. Typically, editorial cartoons accuse, blame, or charge, and occasionally praise or herald, in order to affirm or reorient readers' opinions. Most often, they are thought to defend, criticize, or mock governmental officials and/or policies, or those of other elites and authorities. It is an art form that Mauldin himself used with bite, stating in a 1995 interview that "Every war we've been in after World War II has been a disaster." But in the wake of tragedies, editorial cartoons may serve ceremonial, rather than persuasive, functions, and they often act as a kind of visual obituary following the death of an important person. Such cartoons memorialize through allusions to past tragedies, references to heroism and patriotism, and images of remembrances.

When John F. Kennedy was killed in 1963, Mauldin honored the president with a cartoon that showed a grieving Lincoln Memorial—Lincoln's hair parted in Kennedy's style. Cartoonists Mike Peters and Jack Ohman re-created the tribute for Mauldin: Peters replaced the figure of Lincoln with that of a weeping soldier, and Ohman depicted two crying soldiers—seemingly Willie and Joe—standing beside an equally distraught Lincoln. At least twenty-one more cartoonists re-created Joe and/or Willie to mark Mauldin's passing, each capturing Mauldin's style of heavy lines and dark textures. Six of them featured the iconic dogfaces grieving beside Mauldin's grave, which was most often shown as a combat helmet perched on a fountain pen, in place of a rifle, planted as a grave marker; one showed

Mauldin's combat pen beside Willie and Joe's more traditional battlefield crosses. But perhaps the most representative tribute to Mauldin's importance and influence in cartooning was Milt Priggee's offering: Two combat soldiers walk across clouds, their backs to the reader. The soldier on the left says, "Let's go over to Snoopy's cloud . . . ," referencing the death of Charles Schulz in 2000. The soldier on the right replies, "And quaff a few root beers."

SPARKY AND BILL MAULDIN

JEAN SCHULZ

Most people know my husband as Charles M. Schulz, but to his friends he was always Sparky. Sparky was a twenty-one-year-old machine gunner in the 20th Armored Division at Camp Campbell, Kentucky, when he first saw Bill Mauldin's cartoons in *Stars and Stripes*. Sparky was stunned that a soldier cartoonist, just a little older than he himself, could do such mature work. When Sparky shipped overseas in January of 1945 and saw combat for the first time, his appreciation of Bill's cartoons deepened. Mauldin's characters Willie and Joe got right to the heart of the infantryman's experience of war.

Years later, Sparky became a famous cartoonist in his own right, and in 1969, during the height of the Vietnam War, he drew a special comic for Veterans Day. By this time, Snoopy had become a star of *Peanuts,* which gave Sparky lots of flexibility because of Snoopy's rich imaginative life. Sparky had Snoopy dress up in his WWII Ike jacket and then head over to Bill Mauldin's house to drink root beer.

People have asked, "Why root beer?" Sparky didn't drink, but he liked root beer. *Peanuts* was a family strip, and the humor fit.

Bill Mauldin noticed the Veterans Day tribute to him in the paper and wrote a thank-you note to Sparky. That note started a thirty-year relationship between the two, kept up mostly over the phone and through letters. Sparky loved those phone conversations and would tell me about them from time to time. They were always entertaining, because Bill was a great storyteller.

After years of correspondence, the two of them finally met face-to-face in 1988 when Sparky convinced Bill to attend the Reubens, the National Cartoonists Society's annual award event, in San Francisco. During a ferry ride around the bay, Sparky pulled Bill aside for a private conversation that lasted an hour. Sparky was so excited to have that time with him.

The two men couldn't have been more different. Sparky was reserved and restrained in his manner and lifestyle. Bill, on the other hand, was rowdy and could be gruff. He didn't shy away from conflict and liked to drink. He was a man's man, quite unlike Sparky. Yet the art brought them together.

Their telephone conversations continued, and for the 1999 Reubens in San Antonio, Sparky once again convinced Bill to attend and be on the program. On the night before

Bill's talk, Sparky gathered a dozen of his favorite cartoonist friends to dine with Bill and his ex-wife, Jean. Sparky led Bill in story after story—many of them captured in his book *Up Front*—all the favorite Bill Mauldin moments Sparky had savored for years. It was one of those irreplaceable events that deserved a film crew to capture.

The next day, Bill appeared on the program late in the afternoon. He had been to the bar and made friends with the bartender and wasn't in the best condition to speak. Jean had to finish some of Bill's sentences, because he would lose his train of thought. It was sad. Yet it was also wonderful, because the audience was still spellbound just to be in his presence. When Bill was struggling to tell a story, Sparky jumped up and told it for him. Then a few other older cartoonists, especially the WWII veterans, also stood up and told more Mauldin stories. It defused any tension in the room and turned an awkward situation into a fitting tribute to a great man.

I am glad to relate at least this small memory of a beautiful, unique friendship. Today, in the Charles M. Schulz Museum, a portion of the wall in the permanent gallery is dedicated to the influence of Bill Mauldin on Sparky.

(Copyright © 1969, Peanuts Worldwide LLC.)

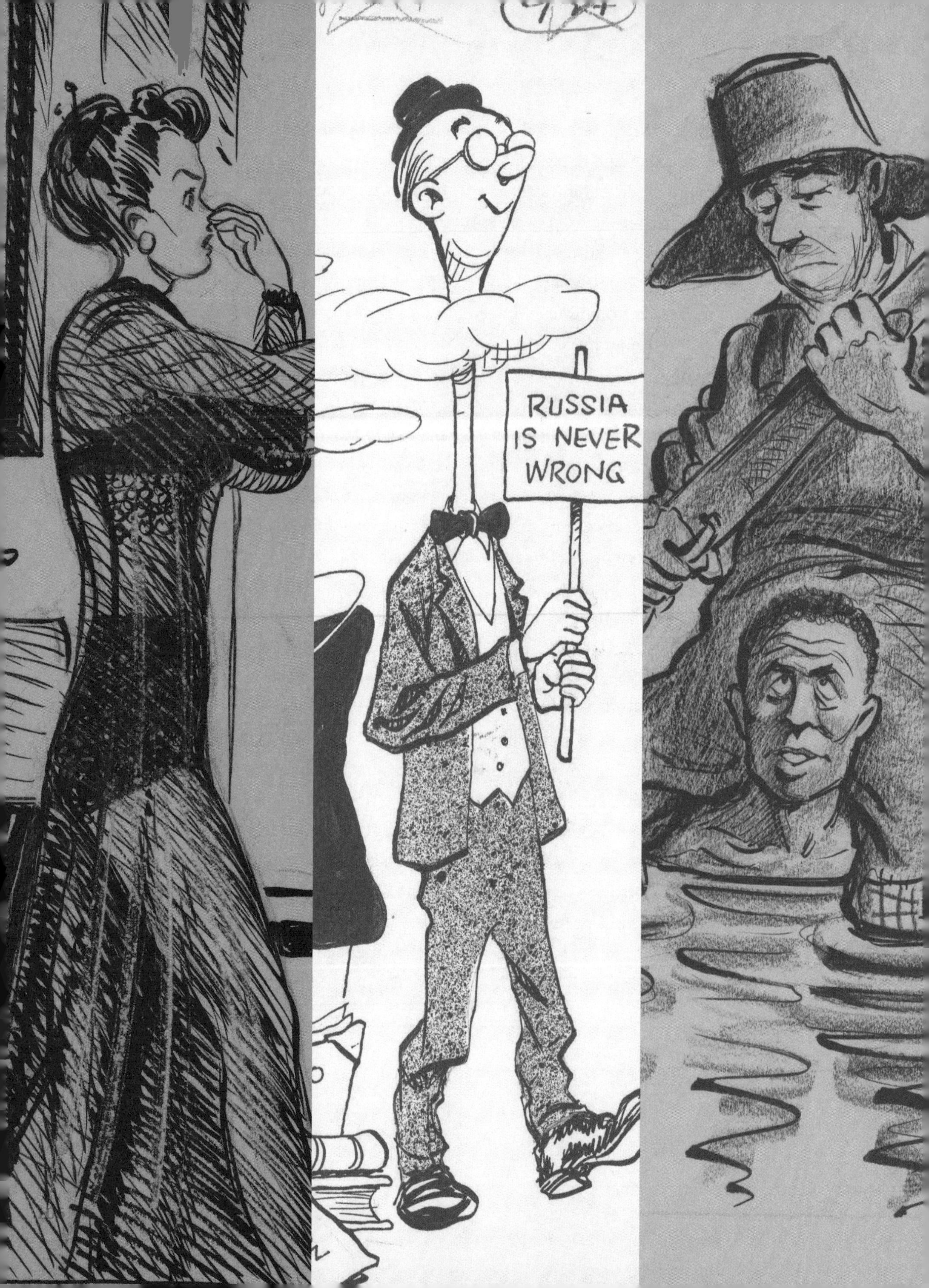
RUSSIA
IS NEVER
WRONG

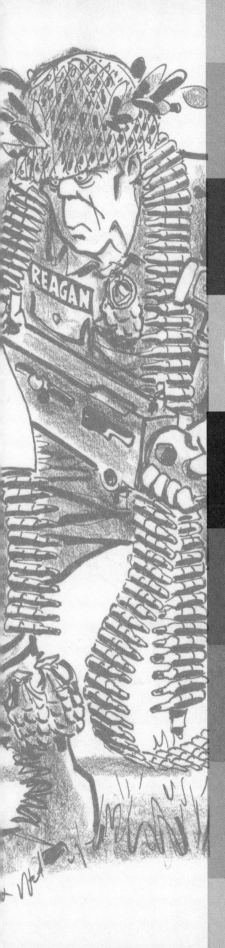

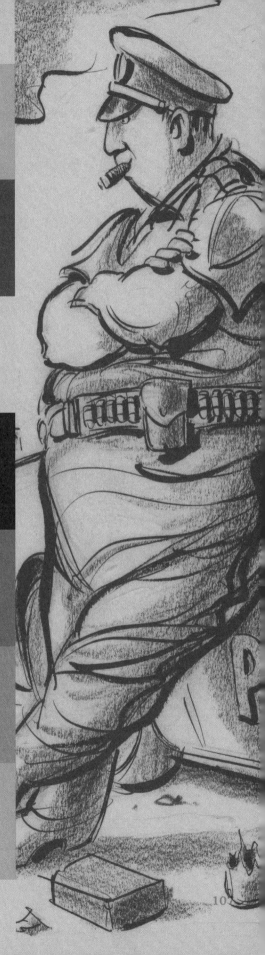

A SELECTION OF BILL MAULDIN'S CARTOONS FROM ►THE PRITZKER◄ MILITARY MUSEUM →& LIBRARY← ►COLLECTIONS◄

"I THINK WE'VE BEEN FIRED UPON, SIR!"

Mauldin created this cartoon in 1939 before completing his course work in life drawing. It relies heavily on the "big foot" style of composition: bold contours and exaggerated human features. At the Chicago Academy of Fine Arts (CAFA), he would refine his style along the more sophisticated lines of Hal Foster's *Tarzan* and Milton Caniff's *Terry and the Pirates.* (Unpublished, 1939.)

"I THINK WE'VE BEEN FIRED UPON, SIR!"

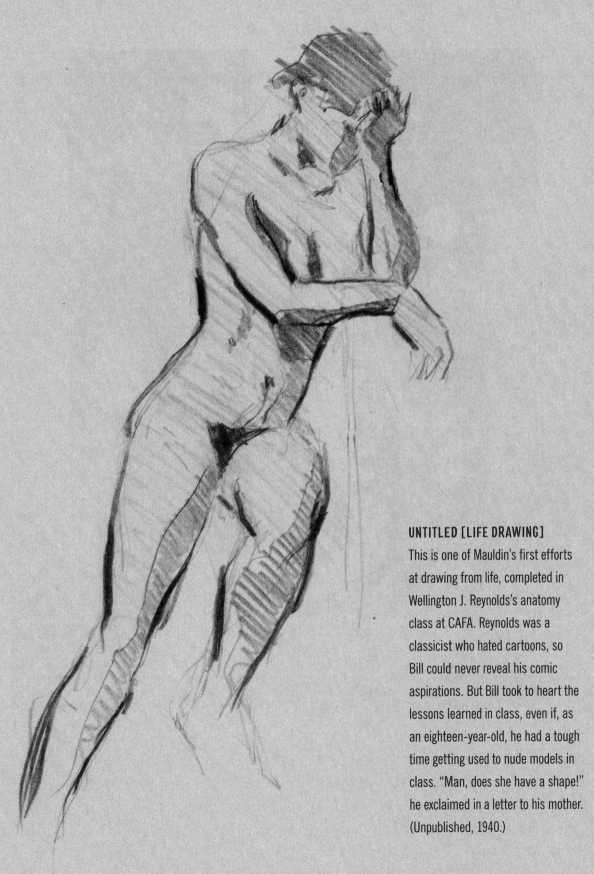

UNTITLED [LIFE DRAWING]
This is one of Mauldin's first efforts at drawing from life, completed in Wellington J. Reynolds's anatomy class at CAFA. Reynolds was a classicist who hated cartoons, so Bill could never reveal his comic aspirations. But Bill took to heart the lessons learned in class, even if, as an eighteen-year-old, he had a tough time getting used to nude models in class. "Man, does she have a shape!" he exclaimed in a letter to his mother. (Unpublished, 1940.)

"WHO'S AFRAID?"

"WHO'S AFRAID?"

This piece, drawn well before Pearl Harbor, gives evidence of a maturing style, as well as Mauldin's strong interventionist views toward war in Europe. Note "Bloody Joe" Stalin in the upper right, a figure of malevolence for Mauldin before Hitler invaded the Soviet Union and the U.S. began supporting "Uncle Joe" in his effort to beat back fascism. (No known publication, 1940–41.)

"I GOT TIRED O' HEARIN' YOU MUGS KICK ABOUT CANNED CREAM IN THE COFFEE!"

"I GOT TIRED O' HEARIN' YOU MUGS KICK ABOUT CANNED CREAM IN THE COFFEE."
Drawn during the Louisiana Maneuvers of 1941, this cartoon was published in Mauldin's first book, *Star*

Spangled Banter, a souvenir collection for soldiers who had participated in the maneuvers. (Originally published in *Star Spangled Banter*, 1941.)

"ALL THE BOYS CHIPPED IN ON IT . . ."
(Originally published in *Star Spangled Banter*, 1941.)

"ALL THE BOYS CHIPPED IN ON IT----"

"Them infantry guys is chucklin' like fiends. We blew up a supply train haulin' overcoats an' blankets to th' Krauts."

"THEM INFANTRY GUYS IS CHUCKLIN' LIKE FIENDS. WE BLEW UP A SUPPLY TRAIN HAULIN' OVERCOATS AN' BLANKETS TO TH' KRAUTS." Artillerymen behind the front lines in Italy in 1944 knew the dire condition of infantrymen who shivered in freezing foxholes without adequate clothing or footwear. In this cartoon, the artillery's objective was no doubt an ammunition train, but the collateral damage of German winter gear inspired *schadenfreude* in American riflemen who envied the enemy's superior winter-weather uniforms. (Originally published in *Stars and Stripes*, 1944.)

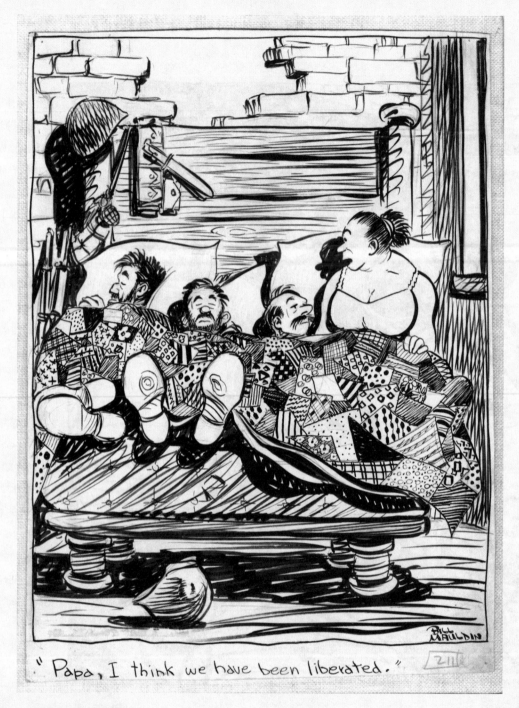

"Papa, I think we have been liberated."

"PAPA, I THINK WE HAVE BEEN LIBERATED."

Infantrymen lived in the ground most of the time but occasionally got access to the comforts of a barn, shed, or, in this case, a farmhouse with the residents still there. (Originally published in *Stars and Stripes,* 1944.)

"Hope I meet that guy in civilian life..."

Z17

"HOPE I MEET THAT GUY IN CIVILIAN LIFE . . ."

The cartoon's caption was a common expression among enlisted men who looked forward to the day they'd return to civilian life and perhaps pay back superiors for any abuse suffered during wartime. Here, a two-star major general with a long military career uses the expression about a three-star who outranks him. (Originally published in *Stars and Stripes,* 1945.)

"SERGEANT, GO REQUISITION THAT FIRE."

Many of Mauldin's cartoons overseas expose how officers used rank to strip basic comforts from enlisted men. It wasn't uncommon for officers to requisition houses, wine casks, and food at the expense of civilians or subordinates. (Originally published in *Stars and Stripes,* 1945.)

"If ya want character references, mister, write to Signor Pasticelli, Venafro, Italy. We occupied his barn for seven weeks."

"IF YA WANT CHARACTER REFERENCES, MISTER, WRITE TO SIGNOR PASTI-CELLI, VENAFRO, ITALY. WE OCCUPIED HIS BARN FOR SEVERAL WEEKS." Mauldin comments on the housing shortage facing veterans after WWII in this cartoon from January 1946. (Originally published by United Feature Syndicate, Inc., 1946.)

"GO ON . . . PLEASE TELL ME THERE'S A WAR ON!"

"Don't you know there's a war on?" was the common rebuke to complaints about the ubiquitous shortages and inconveniences of wartime. Willie, returned from two years on the front lines, is well aware of the war. (Originally published by United Feature Syndicate Inc., 1945.)

SMOKE OLD ROPES

OLD ROPE

NO CIGARETTES
NO CIGARS
NO NOTHIN'

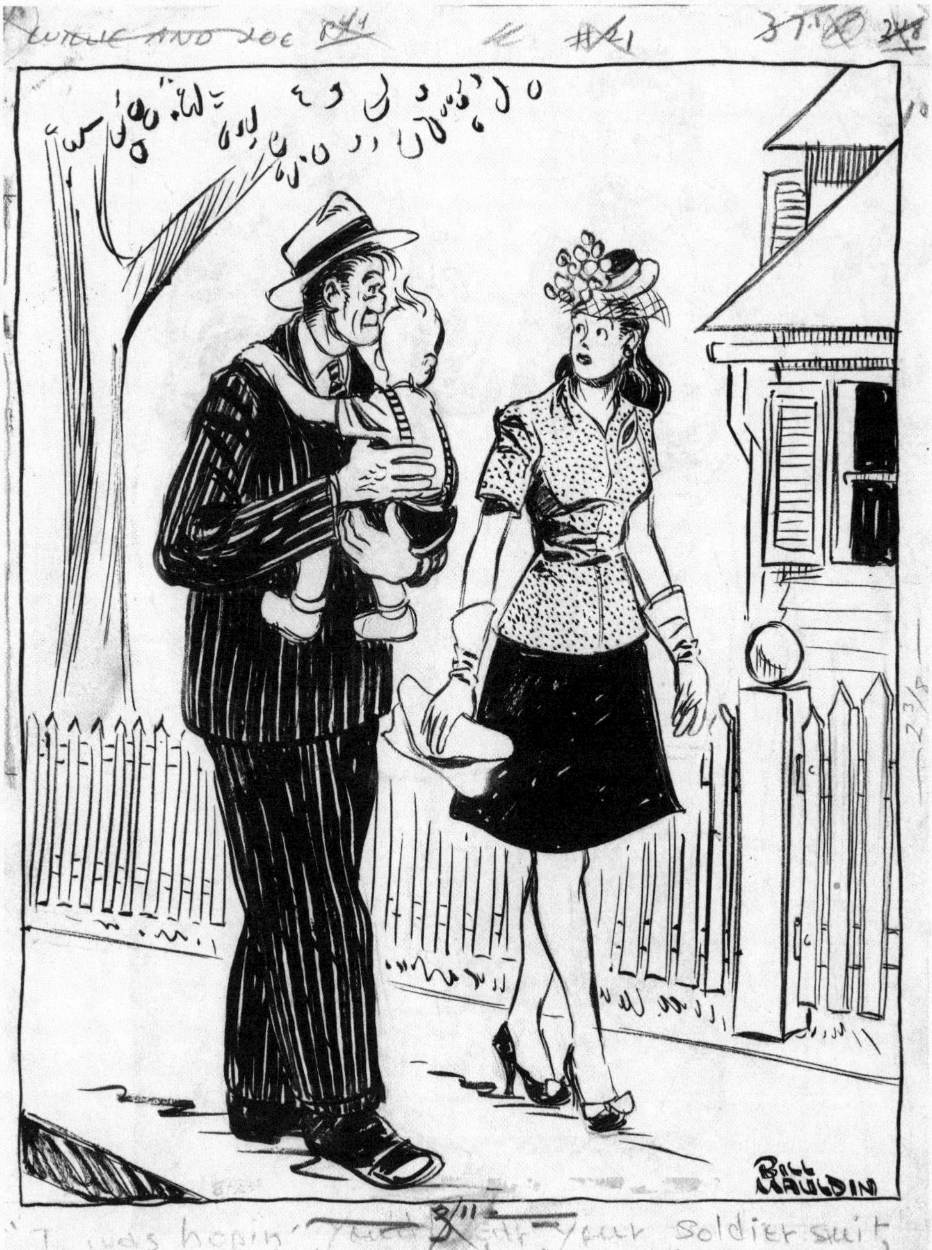
BILL MAULDIN

"I WAS HOPIN' YOU'D WEAR YOUR SOLDIER SUIT, SO I COULD BE PROUD OF YOU."
Though the war was ever present in the minds of those on the home front, civilians nonetheless had little understanding of soldiers who had served in combat on the front-lines. Most discharged servicemen wanted nothing more than to discard their uniforms and enjoy walking around as a civilian again. (Originally published by United Feature Syndicate, Inc., 1945.)

"HER HUSBAND SPENT MONTHS SHOPPING FOR NICE THINGS IN EUROPE, WILLIE. YOU NEVER DID THAT FOR ME."
(Originally published by United Feature Syndicate, Inc., 1945.)

"HIS UNCLE WILLIE MUST BE HOME. HE CALLED ME A DAMN BRASS HAT."
"Brass hat" was sling for a high-ranking officer who seemed more ornamental than useful. (Originally published by United Feature Syndicate, Inc., 1945.)

"His Uncle Willie must be home. He called me a damn brass hat."

"HONEY, I'VE ONLY
WORN IT A WEEK."
(Originally published by United
Feature Syndicate, Inc., 1946.)

"Uncle Louie sent you boys a present. Real European cognac."

"UNCLE LOUIE SENT YOU BOYS A PRESENT. REAL EUROPEAN COGNAC." Willie and Joe, like most infantrymen, drank heavily when they could, usually local varieties like Calvados, apple brandy, in Normandy or vermouth in southern Italy. (Originally published by United Feature Syndicate, Inc., 1945.)

"WHO SAID MY MEDALS WOULDN'T BUY ME A CUPPA COFFEE?"
(Originally published by United Feature Syndicate, Inc., 1945.)

"DERN TOOTIN' IT'S REALISTIC. GIMME MY MONEY BACK!"
Note the "San Pietro" on the box office sign. Mauldin admired the unflinching realism of John Huston's path-breaking documentary, "The Battle of San Pietro", filmed in December 1943 north of Naples, Italy. (Originally published by United Feature Syndicate, Inc., 1945.)

"UGH."

In 1944, Gerald L. K. Smith ran for President of the United States as a member of the anti-immigrant America First Party. The party was notoriously anti-Semitic and nativist and supported racial segregation. Smith and America First grabbed headlines in 1945 as the United States debated the admission of Europe's Displaced Persons into the country. A native of New Mexico, Mauldin had grown up drawing cartoon Native Americans. Here, they lampoon Smith's anti-immigrant position. (Originally published by United Feature Syndicate, Inc., 1945.)

"Ugh."

"Shut up, kid. You got no business discussin' serious matters."

"SHUT UP, KID. YOU GOT NO BUSINESS DISCUSSIN' SERIOUS MATTERS."

It's hard to believe today, but after WWII, some returning veterans felt shut out of organizations like the American Legion and the VFW, which were largely run by older WWI veterans. Mauldin eventually became active in the short-lived American Veterans Committee, which represented young WWII veterans. (Originally published by United Feature Syndicate, Inc., 1945.)

"I unnerstand our congressmen are worryin' about democracy in th' Balkans."

← "I UNNERSTAND OUR CONGRESSMEN ARE WORRYIN' ABOUT DEMOCRACY IN TH' BALKANS." (Originally published by United Feature Syndicate, Inc., 1945.)

↑ "MOMMY SAYS I GOTTA QUIT SEEIN' YA, BUTCH. YA GOT MINORITIES OR SOMETHIN'." (Originally published by United Feature Syndicate, Inc., 1946.)

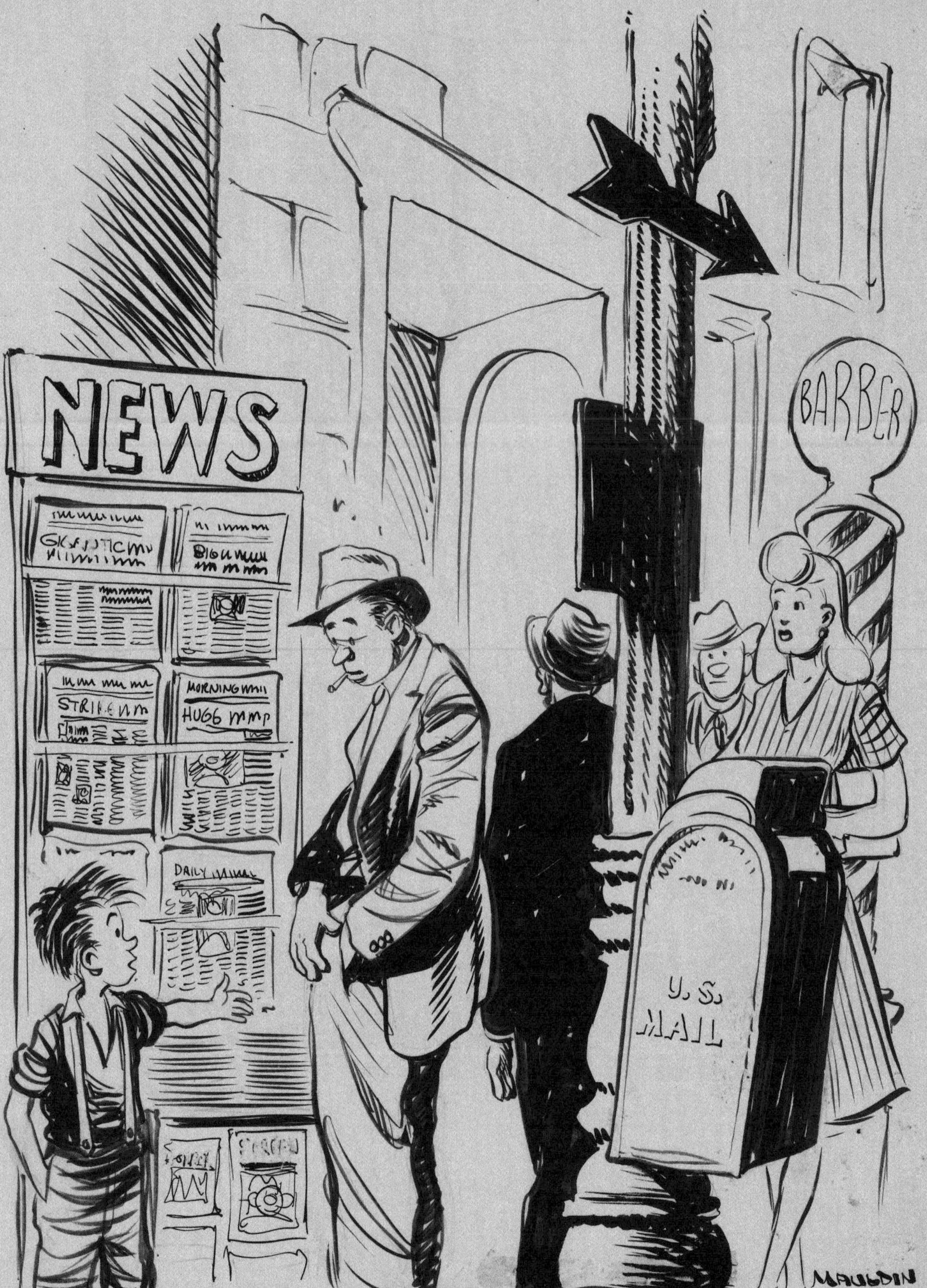
NEWS
MORNING
DAILY
BARBER
U. S.
MAIL
MAULDIN

"It's something silly about the last days of the Roman Empire."

"IT'S SOMETHING SILLY
ABOUT THE LAST DAYS
OF THE ROMAN EMPIRE."
(Originally published by
United Feature Syndicate,
Inc., 1946.)

← "RED, PINK, LEFT OF CENTER, COLORLESS,
CAREFUL, CONSERVATIVE, OR REACTIONARY?"

Pearl Harbor dampened political partisanship "for the duration," as the saying went. But with VJ Day came an explosion of deferred debate, with newspapers of every stripe contesting their visions for postwar America and the globe.
(Originally published by United Feature Syndicate, Inc., 1946.)

". . . WHERE IGNORANCE IS BLISS, 'TIS FOLLY TO BE WISE."

Mauldin came home from war with warm feelings for the Soviets, who had suffered unimaginable casualties at the hands of the Wehrmacht. By 1946, however, Soviet aggression and authoritarianism in Eastern Europe turned him against the U.S.'s erstwhile ally. He came to see the Left as ignorant as the Right. (Originally published by United Feature Syndicate, Inc., 1946.)

" ... where ignorance is bliss, 'tis folly to be wise

"YER A MENACE TO THE PEOPLE.
IT'S ME DUTY TO SINK YOUR END OF THE BOAT."

(Originally published by United Feature Syndicate, Inc., 1947.)

"I'D SWEAR HE LICKED HIS CHOPS AS WE WENT BY."
When the Selective Training and Service Act expired in 1947, the nation went to an all-volunteer military for the first time since 1940. The Draft would ultimately be reinstated in 1948. (Originally published by United Feature Syndicate, Inc., 1947.)

RECRUITING

YOU'LL LIKE THE NEW ARMY

"I'd swear he licked his chops as we went by."

"WE A'INT NO LOST GENERATION. WE JUST BEEN MISLAID."

(Originally published by United Feature Syndicate, Inc., 1947.)

UNTITLED [GENERALS]

Soviet officers' zeal for festooning their chests with medals struck Mauldin as a perverse repudiation of the egalitarian ideal of Communism. American General Frank Howley observed Soviet General Georgy Zhukov in Berlin after the war: "Across his chest, and almost down below his hips, hung so many decorations that a special brass plate had to be worn to house this immense collection, giving the impression of being riveted to the Russian's chest. . . . In an emergency, he had hung one decoration, a gold saucer affair, on his right hip." (Originally published by United Feature Syndicate, Inc., 1947.)

"INVESTIGATE <u>THEM</u>?
HECK, THAT'S MAH POSSE."
(Originally published by United
Feature Syndicate, Inc., 1947.)

"THEM OLD EAGLES SURE SPOIL THAT NEW UNIFORM, COLONEL."

The year 1947 was a turning point in the history of civil rights. Not only did Jackie Robinson break the color barrier in baseball, but an advisory commission on universal military training recommended to President Harry S. Truman that the armed forces be desegregated. Mauldin applauded the effort. On July 26, 1948, President Truman issued Executive Order 9981, which declared "that there shall be equality of treatment and opportunity for all persons in the armed services without regard to race, color, religion or national origin." (Originally published by United Feature Syndicate, Inc., 1947.)

"Them old eagles sure spoil that new uniform, colonel."

HEAD OF THE HOUSEHOLD

Mauldin loved automobiles and religiously washed and waxed his own collection of vehicles on Saturday afternoons. Yet he was a fierce critic of the American postwar car culture, which he saw as an expensive fetish that harmed the nation's social fabric and the environment. (Originally published in the *St. Louis Post-Dispatch*, 1960.)

©1960 St. Louis Post-Dispatch

HEAD OF THE HOUSEHOLD

"I LOVE THY ROCKS AND RILLS..."

©1960 St. Louis Post-Dispatch

MAULDIN

"I LOVE THY ROCKS AND RILLS . . ."

An early advocate of environmentalism, conservation, and antipollution efforts, Mauldin quotes from the second verse of Samuel Francis Smith's lyrics to "America (My Country, 'Tis of Thee)." (Originally published in the *St. Louis Post-Dispatch,* 1960.)

"I'M NOT PLAYING HOOKY. I FELL OUT."

"I'M NOT PLAYING HOOKY. I FELL OUT."

Though he never graduated high school, Mauldin supported increased federal funding for public education. (Originally published in the *St. Louis Post-Dispatch,* 1960.)

"IT'S POSITIVELY FRIGHTENING! THESE HANDS CAN CHANGE HISTORY."

"BLOOD, SWEAT, AND TEARS, ANYONE?"
In 1940, Winston Churchill had rallied the British nation to war against Germany, offering nothing "but blood, toil, tears and sweat." Two decades later, on January 20, 1961, John F. Kennedy's Inaugural Address issued a similarly rousing call to Cold War action, appealing to Americans to "pay any price, bear any burden, meet any hardship, support any friend, oppose any foe to assure the survival and success of liberty." (Originally published in the *St. Louis Post-Dispatch*, 1961.) ➡

"BLOOD, SWEAT, AND TEARS, ANYONE?"

⬅ **"IT'S POSITIVELY FRIGHTENING! THESE HANDS CAN CHANGE HISTORY."**

Mauldin drew this cartoon on October 20, 1960, in anticipation of the fourth and final televised debate between presidential candidates John F. Kennedy and Richard M. Nixon scheduled for the next day. Three weeks earlier, in the first televised debate in history, a visibly ill Nixon had shown up looking pale and tired. Sweat had beaded on his face, and whatever makeup he had used only accentuated his five o'clock shadow. More than 70 million Americans had watched the debates and gave a tanned and fit-looking Kennedy the edge.
(Originally published in the *St. Louis Post-Dispatch,* 1960.)

"EAT, DRINK, AND BE MERRY, FOR TOMORROW YOU MAY BE NON-DEDUCTIBLE."

← **"EAT, DRINK, AND BE MERRY, FOR TOMORROW YOU MAY BE NON-DEDUCTIBLE."** President Kennedy came into office promising to reform the tax code. Proposals and counter-proposals ranged widely for years until the passing of the United States Revenue Act of 1964, which, indeed, eliminated some deductions even as it lowered rates and introduced the standard deduction. (Originally published in the *St. Louis Post-Dispatch*, 1961.)

"GOOD NEWS, MEN — WE'RE GOING BACK TO CIVILIZED WARFARE!"

"GOOD NEWS, MEN—WE'RE GOING BACK TO CIVILIZED WARFARE!"

President Eisenhower's New Look military relied heavily on nuclear deterrents, even in the face of small conflicts or "brushfires." President Kennedy immediately changed this policy, preferring Flexible Response, which would allow Americans to engage in smaller regional conflicts without threatening thermonuclear war. (Originally published in the *St. Louis Post-Dispatch*, 1961.)

"LET ME TAKE YOU AWAY FROM ALL THIS." South Korea (Republic of Korea) descended into chaos in 1960, as street demonstrations overthrew the corrupt presidency of Syngman Rhee, and then a military coup led by General Park Chung-hee seized power the following year from a new democratically elected government. Meanwhile, the Communist autocracy of North Korea (Democratic People's Republic of Korea) entered a period of stability, industrialization, and relative prosperity. (Originally published in the *St. Louis Post-Dispatch*, 1961.)

"LET ME TAKE YOU AWAY FROM ALL THIS."

"IT SOUNDED LIKE A TRACTOR, BUT IT WAS ONLY A TRUCK GOING BY."

"IT SOUNDED LIKE A TRACTOR, BUT IT WAS ONLY A TRUCK GOING BY."

On April 15, 1961, 1,500 CIA-trained Cuban exiles opposed to Fidel Castro launched a disastrous invasion of Cuba in the Bahía de Cochinos, or Bay of Pigs. Over a thousand of the invaders were captured and held prisoner by Cuba. Castro offered to return the POWs for 500 large tractors. Kennedy created the "Tractors for Freedom Committee" to support the exchange. After a year and a half of negotiations, Cuba returned the prisoners for $53 million in food and medicine, raised by private funds. (Originally published in the *St. Louis Post-Dispatch*, 1961.)

"YOU FIRST, JACK."

"YOU FIRST, JACK."

In July 1961, when this cartoon appeared, the Cold War standoff between the US and USSR was escalating rapidly. The tense meeting in Vienna the previous month between Soviet leader Nikita Khrushchev and President John F. Kennedy had only magnified disagreements over West Berlin, Cuba, Laos and other parts of the world where the super-powers had armed proxies facing each other off. As relations deteriorated, both sides stepped back from ongoing negotiations to curb the testing of nuclear weapons. Both the US and USSR had respected a test-ing moratorium since 1958 as they worked toward an agreement on a permanent ban. The moratorium meant the world enjoyed a three-year respite from nuclear tests that heightened the arms race and contaminated the environment. In June 1961, Kennedy grew wary that the Soviets were planning to test a new hydrogen bomb. The Soviets saw that Kennedy's suspicions might prompt him to renew the US's own tests. The stalemate broke in September, which both sides began testing nuclear weapons again. Two years later, the Cold War rivals finally signed a Limited Nuclear Test Ban Treaty. (Originally published in the *St. Louis Post-Dispatch*, 1961.)

"WHAT HAPPENED TO YOU?"

The Kennedy administration claimed victory in April 1962
when the President, irate at steel companies for their plans
to hike prices by $6 per ton, publicly shamed the industry
into rescinding the increases. Fearing a "wage-price spiral"
that might propel inflation, JFK then turned to working with
unions to keep wage demands in line with prices.
(Originally published in the *St. Louis Post-Dispatch*, 1962.)

MAULDIN
©1962 St. Louis Post-Dispatch

32
(61) R

"WHAT HAPPENED TO YOU?"

5/6/62

© 1962 Field Enterprises, Inc.

MAULDIN
Oxford, Miss.

"AIN'T THEM FUN-LOVIN' SCHOOLBOYS A RIOT?"

"AIN'T THEM FUN-LOVIN' SCHOOLBOYS A RIOT?"
Mauldin flew from Chicago to Oxford, Mississippi, on September 29, 1962, in anticipation of the arrival of James Meredith, who was scheduled to enroll as the University of Mississippi's first African American student. The next day, the campus erupted in riot, as white students rebelled against the prospect of desegregating Ole Miss. Three people were killed and hundreds injured while local and state police did little to stop it and then abandoned the scene. (Originally published by Field Enterprises, Inc., 1962.)

"INFURIATING LITTLE DEVIL, ISN'T HE?"
Weeks before the United States discovered the missiles in Cuba that would lead to the October Missile Crisis, the Soviet Union began shipping mysterious cargo to the Communist island nation. The Soviets made a big show to warn that if the U.S. were to attack Cuba, "this will be the beginning of unleashing war . . . which might plunge the world into the disaster of a universal world war with the use of thermonuclear weapons." (Originally published by Field Enterprises, Inc., 1962.)

"INFURIATING LITTLE DEVIL, ISN'T HE?"

"YOU AIN'T GAINING MUCH ALTITUDE HOLDING ME DOWN."

"ISN'T SCIENCE WONDERFUL?"

"ISN'T
SCIENCE WONDERFUL?"
The United States and Soviet Union
signed the "Memorandum of Understanding
Regarding the Establishment of a Direct Communications
Line", creating a "hotline" between the Pentagon and the Kremlin. The
hotline (actually, a teletype) was intended to provide direct, instant communication
between the two superpowers in case of a crisis. The prior fall, during the October Missile Crisis,
it took the U.S. twelve hours to receive and decrypt critical messages from Soviet Premier Nikita Khrushchev.
(Originally published in the *Chicago Sun-Times*, 1963.)

"I MUST HAVE STRUCK A NERVE."

Mauldin drew this cartoon on August 6, 1964, immediately after a major turning point in the Vietnam War, the Gulf of Tonkin Incident. On August 2, the USS *Maddox* exchanged fire with North Vietnamese torpedo boats while patrolling off the coast of North Vietnam. Two days later, the *Maddox* returned to the area with a second destroyer, the USS *Turner Joy*. The *Maddox* reported being fired upon again, this time in international waters. The Lyndon Johnson administration used this second attack as the justification to launch air raids the following day and to call for expanded executive war-making powers (the Gulf of Tonkin Resolution). Mauldin supported the retaliatory strikes. He, like most Americans, didn't know that the second attack on the *Maddox* hadn't actually occurred. The torpedoes reported by the *Maddox* crew were, in fact, false radar images in heavy seas. (Originally published in the *Chicago Sun-Times*, 1964.)

"IT'S GETTING SO BAD THAT EVEN PEOPLE ARE COMPLAINING."
(Originally published in the *Chicago Sun-Times*, 1965.) ➡

"I MUST HAVE STRUCK A NERVE."

"IT'S GETTING SO BAD THAT EVEN PEOPLE ARE COMPLAINING."

BULLDOGGER

In 1966, Mauldin encapsulated the dilemma facing Lyndon Johnson, one that would trigger his downfall. As Johnson put it in his post–White House memoir, "I knew from the start that I was bound to be crucified either way I moved. If I left the woman I really loved—the Great Society—in order to get involved with that bitch of a war on the other side of the world, then I would lose everything at home. All my programs. All my hopes to feed the hungry and shelter the homeless. All my dreams to provide education and medical care. . . . But if I left that war and let the Communists take over South Vietnam, then I would be seen as a coward and my nation would be seen as an appeaser, and we would both find it impossible to accomplish anything for anybody anywhere on the entire globe." (Originally published in the *Chicago Sun-Times*, 1966.)

"YOUNG MAN, YOU'VE GOT NOTHING THERE BUT WEEDS!"
(Originally published in the *Chicago Sun-Times*, 1967.) ➡

BULLDOGGER

"YOUNG MAN, YOU'VE GOT NOTHING THERE BUT WEEDS!"

"I CAN'T DECIDE WHICH WAY IS MOST BECOMING . . ."
(Originally published in the *Chicago Sun-Times*, 1966.)

"I CAN'T DECIDE WHICH WAY IS MOST BECOMING..."

Mauldin frequently used puppets, especially with Mao as puppeteer, as a way of explaining the alliances of Communist nations. It was a simplistic image, though Mauldin skillfully suggests North Korean dictator Kim Il-Sung's reluctance for military adventure against U.S. forces in Vietnam, as well as his wary attitude toward China. (Originally published in the *Chicago Sun-Times*, 1966.)

"AREN'T YOU GOING TO HELP YOUR LITTLE PAL?"

"WELCOME TO THE GREAT SOCIETY."

1965

1967

WAR IN VIETNAM, 1965/1967
(Originally published
in the *Chicago
Sun-Times*, 1967.)

News Item: L.B.J. THINKS CARTOONISTS MISTREAT HIS NOSE

Personally, I always use calipers to draw him.

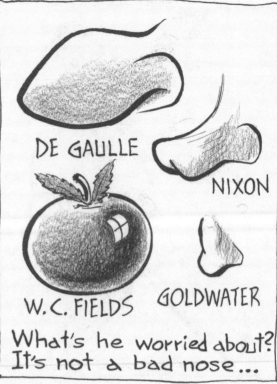

DE GAULLE

NIXON

W.C. FIELDS

GOLDWATER

What's he worried about? It's not a bad nose...

Maybe he'd like us to **DE**-exaggerate it.

Johnson does admit that he has big ears. Does this give us carte blanche?

MAULDIN
©1968 Chicago Sun-Times

NEWS ITEM: L.B.J. THINKS CARTOONISTS MISTREAT HIS NOSE.
(Originally published in the *Chicago Sun-Times*, 1968.)

"THE ODD THING ABOUT ASSASSINS, DR. KING, IS THAT THEY THINK THEY'VE KILLED YOU."
This was Mauldin's tribute to Rev. Martin Luther King Jr. after his assassination on April 4, 1968. Twenty years earlier, Mahatma Gandhi was assassinated by a Hindu nationalist after leading India to independence through the kind of nonviolent resistance advocated by King. (Originally published in the *Chicago Sun-Times*, 1968.)

"THE ODD THING ABOUT ASSASSINS, DR. KING, IS THAT THEY THINK THEY'VE KILLED YOU."

PLEASE RETURN WALLET TO
Lyndon B. Johnson
1400 Pennsylvania
Washin

VIET NAM

©1968 Chicago Sun-Times

BOOKENDS?

In March 1968, Robert F. Kennedy announced his candidacy for the Democratic Party's nomination to replace fellow Democrat Lyndon Johnson. LBJ loathed RFK and shuddered at the prospect of another Kennedy in the White House. "The thing that I had feared from the first day of my Presidency was actually coming true," Johnson wrote during his Texas retirement. "Robert Kennedy had openly announced his intention to reclaim the throne in the memory of his brother. And the American people, swayed by the magic of his name, were dancing in the streets." (Originally published in the *Chicago Sun-Times,* 1968.)

UNTITLED [EMPTY WALLET]
(Originally published in the *Chicago Sun-Times,* 1968.)

BOOKENDS?

BOOKMARKS

Mauldin drew this cartoon on June 6, 1968. In the early hours of
that day, forty-two-year-old Senator Robert F. Kennedy died in the
Good Samaritan Hospital in Los Angeles after being shot on June 5
at the Ambassador Hotel by assassin Sirhan Sirhan. Following on
the heels of Martin Luther King Jr.'s assassination two months earlier, RFK's
assassination triggered national
soul-searching about the role
of violence in American
history and society.
(Originally published
in the *Chicago
Sun-Times*,
1968.)

BOOKMARKS

"I'D LIKE TO WITHDRAW MY REQUEST FOR A WEEKEND PASS IN SAIGON."

"THEY'RE DISRUPTIVE, OUTRAGEOUS, ARROGANT, UNREASONABLE, OBNOXIOUS, IDEALISTIC, ENTHUSIASTIC.....AND YOUTHFUL. THAT REALLY HURTS, DOESN'T IT?"

← "THEY'RE DIS-RUPTIVE, OUTRAGEOUS, ARROGANT, UNREASON-ABLE, OBNOXIOUS, IDE-ALISTIC, ENTHUSIASTIC . . . AND YOUTHFUL. THAT REALLY HURTS, DOESN'T IT?" (Originally published in the *Chicago Sun-Times*, 1968.)

"I'M SURE I THREW IT SOMEWHERE IN HERE..."

"I'M SURE I THREW IT SOMEWHERE IN HERE . . ."

Mauldin didn't care for French president Charles de Gaulle, who was an obstreperous ally of the United States. In 1966, the president had sent a shocking memo to the U.S., announcing his country's withdrawal from the integrated military alliance of the North Atlantic Treaty Organization (NATO), designed as a bulwark against the Soviet Union's Eastern Bloc. After the Soviet Union's invasion of Czecho-slovakia in 1968, however, de Gaulle emphasized France's continued partnership with NATO. (Originally published in the *Chicago Sun-Times,* 1968.)

"I'M SURE THEY DID ONLY WHAT WAS NECESSARY TO PRESERVE LAW AND ORDER."

THE PEDDLER ➡

In 1969, Congress debated banning from the airwaves the largest advertiser on television: tobacco companies. A year after this cartoon, President Nixon signed into law the Public Health Cigarette Smoking Act, which forbade cigarette advertising on TV and radio and required cigarette packages carry the statement "Warning: The Surgeon General Has Determined That Cigarette Smoking Is Dangerous to Your Health" (Originally published in the *Chicago Sun-Times*, 1969.)

"I'M SURE THEY DID ONLY WHAT WAS NECESSARY TO PRESERVE LAW AND ORDER."

Richard Nixon was the "law and order" candidate in the Presidential election of 1968. That same year, the Soviet Union with Warsaw Pact allies invaded Czechoslovakia to put an end to Alexander Bubček's Prague Spring liberalization reforms that promised "Socialism with a Human Face." The day before Mauldin created this cartoon, a student activist named Jan Palach set himself on fire in Prague in protest of the Soviet occupation. His funeral unleashed the last major demonstration in Czechoslovakia until the Velvet Revolution of 1989. (Originally published in the *Chicago Sun-Times*, 1969.)

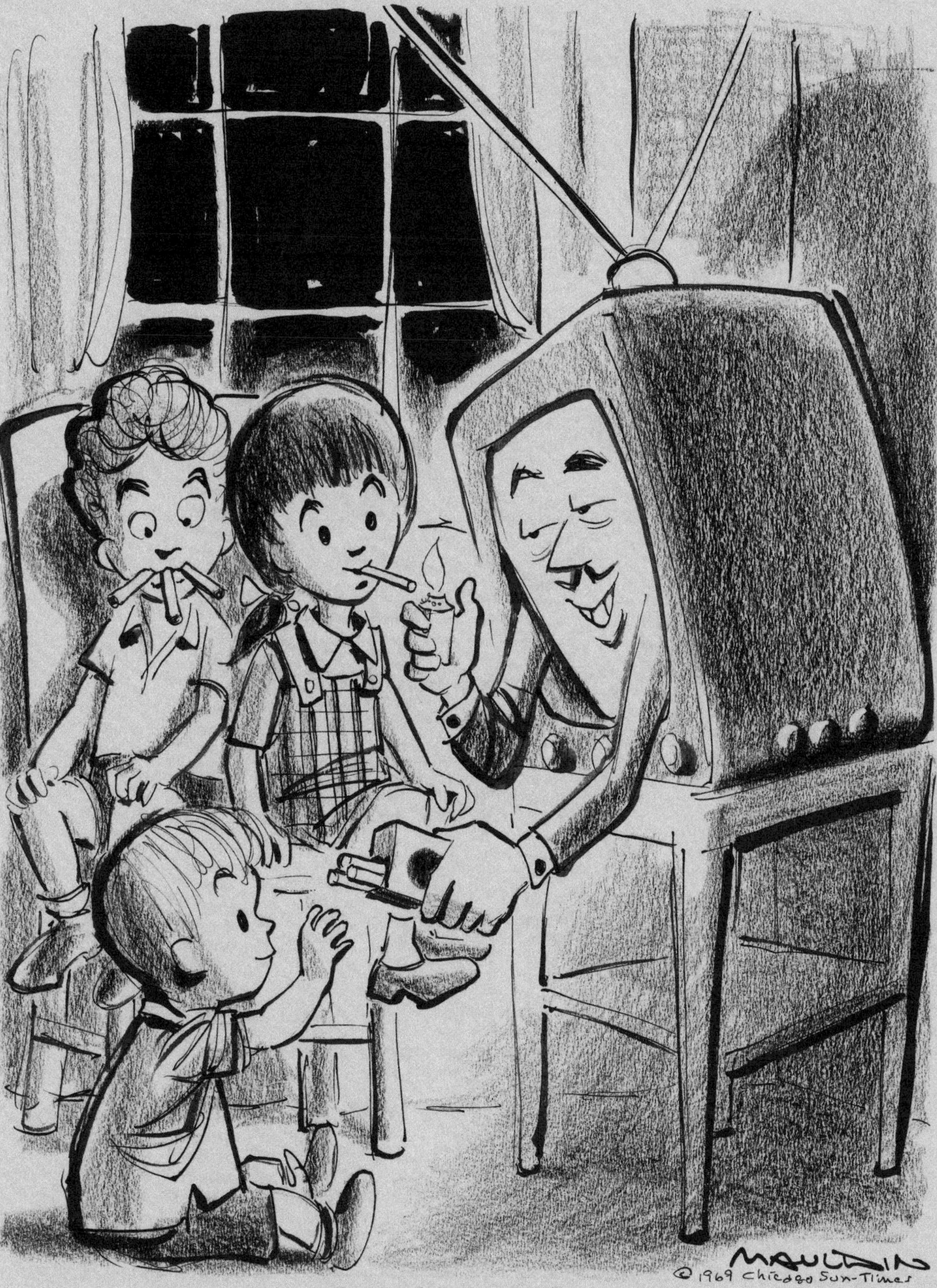
MAULDIN
© 1969 Chicago Sun-Times

THE PEDDLER

"THAT CAT'S ON CRAB GRASS." ➡️ (Originally published in the *Chicago Sun-Times*, 1969.)

"HE'S MY ONLY CHILD. PLEASE GET HIM OFF THE CAMPUS."

"HE'S MY ONLY CHILD. PLEASE GET HIM OFF THE CAMPUS."

In May 1969, college campuses erupted in violence as baton-wielding police clashed with demonstrators who protested the Vietnam War, racism, and other grievances. By then, student activists had grown more militant, and sit-ins and campus building takeovers occurred all over the country, from Harvard and Stanford to Purdue and North Carolina A&T. (Originally published in the *Chicago Sun-Times,* 1969.)

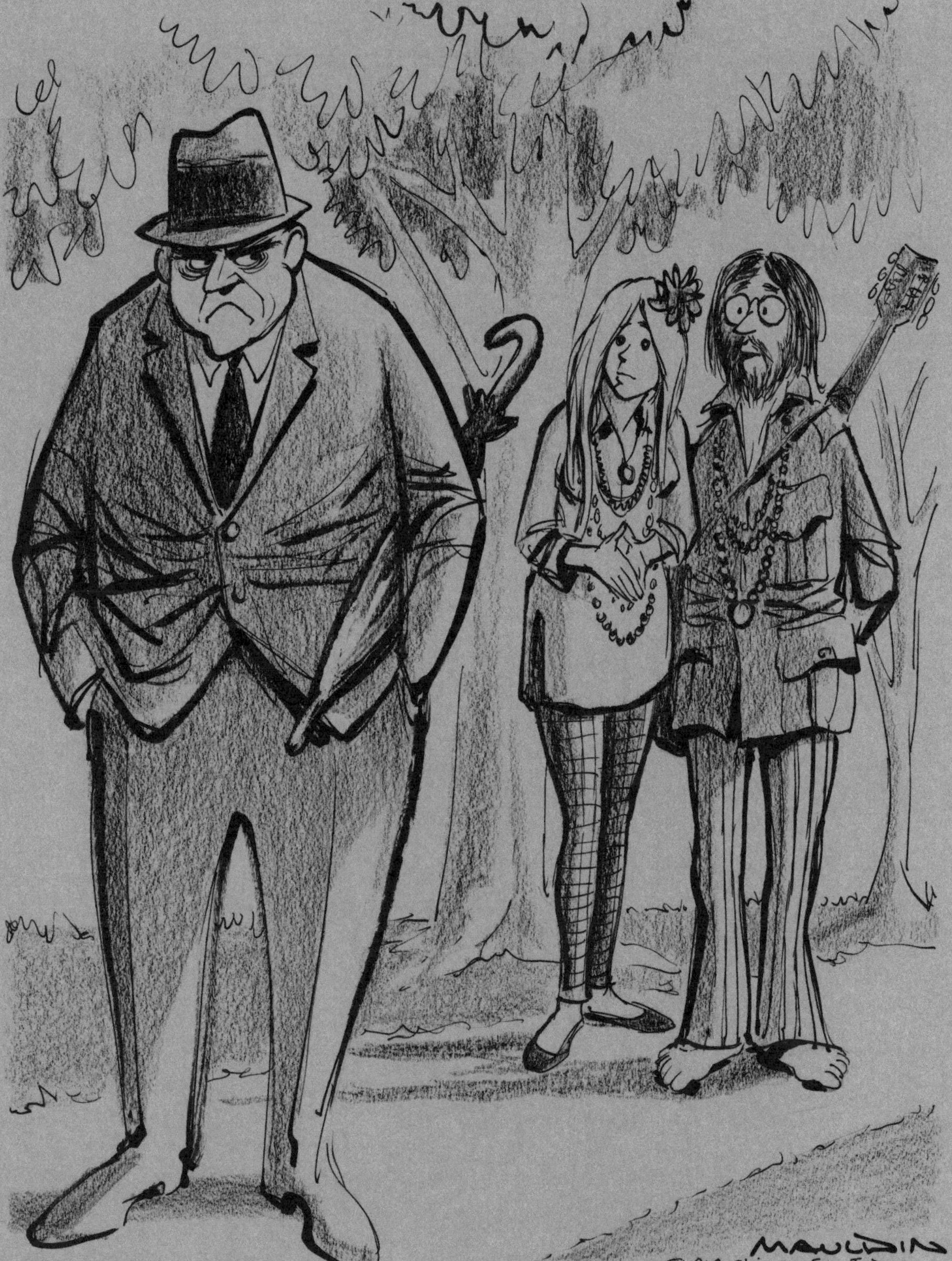
MAULDIN
© 1969 Chicago Sun-Times

"THAT CAT'S ON CRAB GRASS."

"THAT'S THE ANTI-ESTABLISHMENT ESTABLISHMENT."
Mauldin often used children to capture the ironies of the adult world. Here, on the eve of Woodstock, kids note that the counterculture has entered the mainstream. (Originally published in the *Chicago Sun-Times*, 1969.)

"THAT'S THE ANTI-ESTABLISHMENT ESTABLISHMENT."

DING-A-LINGS

DING-A-LINGS

In August 1968 during the Democratic National Convention, Chicago mayor Richard J. Daley oversaw a widely condemned "police riot" against antiwar demonstrators. The following year, the week before this cartoon came out, Students for a Democratic Society, under the leadership of radical militants called the Weathermen, launched "Days of Rage," intended to "Bring the War Home" to Chicago. Activists smashed storefronts, battled police, and set off a bomb in Haymarket Square. (Originally published in the *Chicago Sun-Times,* 1969.)

"MOON, HELL—
THIS IS SOUTHEAST ASIA."
(Originally published in the
Chicago Sun-Times, 1971.)

Chicago Sun-Times   ©1971 MAULDIN

"MOON, HELL—THIS IS SOUTHEAST ASIA."

"I ONLY TAP PEOPLE WHO DESERVE IT."

In March 1971, Americans began to learn for about a massive domestic surveillance program under the direction of J. Edgar Hoover's FBI. Called COINTELPRO (Counter Intelligence Program), it relied on illegal means to "expose, disrupt, misdirect, discredit, or otherwise neutralize" scores of liberal and left-wing people and groups, including Martin Luther King Jr. and civil rights organizations. (Originally published in the *Chicago Sun-Times,* 1971.)

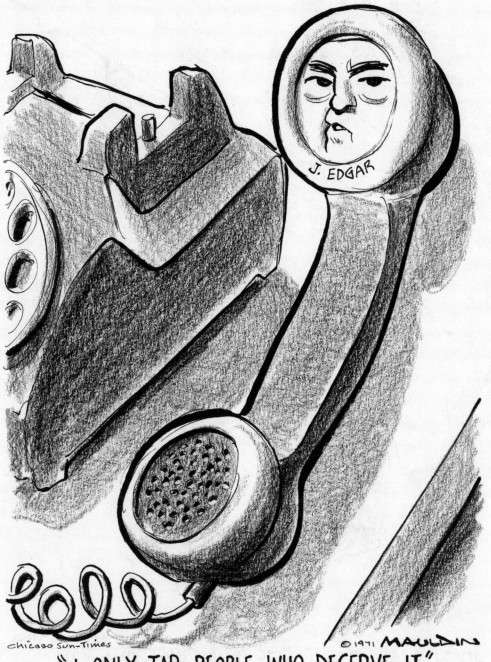

Chicago Sun-Times   ©1971 MAULDIN

"I ONLY TAP PEOPLE WHO DESERVE IT."

"THE HOLE IS ABOUT THE SIZE OF A PING-PONG BALL."
On April 10, 1971, fifteen U.S. table tennis players crossed into mainland China at the invitation of Chairman Mao for a ten-day tour. It was the first time a delegation of Americans had visited China since the Communist Revolution of 1949. This "Ping-Pong Diplomacy" initiated a thaw between the United States and China, culminating in President Richard Nixon's historic visit the following February. (Originally published in the *Chicago Sun-Times*, 1971.)

Chicago Sun-Times   ©1971 MAULDIN

"THE HOLE IS ABOUT THE SIZE OF A PING-PONG BALL."

"CAMERAS, AUTOMOBILES—WHY CAN'T THEY LEAVE A MINK COAT?"

(Originally published in the *Chicago Sun-Times*, 1971.)

"WE'VE BOMBED EVERYTHING BUT SAIGON — MAYBE THAT'S THE ANSWER."

← **"WE'VE BOMBED EVERYTHING BUT SAIGON— MAYBE THAT'S THE ANSWER."**

With a crazed look in his eyes, President Nixon considers bombing his own allies in Saigon on December 17, 1972. In reality, Nixon initiated the following day the infamous "Christmas Bombings" (Operation Linebacker II), designed to force the North Vietnamese back to negotiations. Over the course of the next twelve days, 729 B-52 sorties pummeled targets in North Vietnam, the largest bombing campaign since World War II. Nixon deliberately projected to the enemy an image of himself as unstable and irrational in his penchant for violence. "I call it the Madman Theory," he told an advisor. North Vietnam did return to the bargaining table, which quickly resulted in the Paris Peace Accords on January 27, 1973, ending U.S. involvement in Vietnam. But the biggest obstacle to the peace treaty all along wasn't North Vietnam. Rather, it was the U.S.'s ally in Saigon. The South Vietnamese government correctly surmised that a U.S. exit would doom Saigon to a Communist takeover. (Originally published in the *Chicago Sun-Times,* 1972.)

"THE COMMANDER-IN-CHIEF WANTS US TO MISS LITTLE GIRLS."

On June 8, 1972, AP photographer Nick Ut snapped a photograph of nine-year-old Kim Phúc running naked down a street in Tràng Bàng, South Vietnam, after a napalm attack that burned her back. The photo horrified the world and highlighted the carnage wrought by the war upon civilians. By this time, American forces on the ground in Vietnam had dwindled to a tiny fraction of their 1969 peak, but the Nixon administration had drastically ramped up U.S. air support for South Vietnamese ground forces. Mauldin understood the futility of trying to wage war in Vietnam, especially an air war, without injuring or impacting civilian bystanders. (Originally published in the *Chicago Sun-Times,* 1972.)

"THE COMMANDER-IN-CHIEF WANTS US TO MISS LITTLE GIRLS."

UNTITLED

[E PLURIBUS UNUM]

With Vice President
Spiro Agnew under indictment
for bribery, extortion, and tax
evasion and President Nixon under
investigation for his role in the Watergate
break-in and cover-up, the eagle in the Great Seal of
the United States hides his face in shame. Mauldin often
said the best cartoons don't need captions.

(Originally published in the *Chicago Sun-Times,* 1973.)

"VICIOUS, MALICIOUS DISTORTION!"

"VICIOUS, MALICIOUS DISTORTION!"
(Originally published in the
Chicago Sun-Times, 1973.)

"THIS DAMN TEEPEE LEAKS."

This cartoon from 1973 plays on Mauldin's well-known wartime cartoon and GI comic book titled, *This Damn Tree Leaks* from almost thirty years earlier. At a time when the Nixon administration was trying to diffuse the situation at Wounded Knee over Native rights, Mauldin not so subtly reminds his readers of the deceit and dishonor that characterized the history of U.S. federal relations with Native American tribes. (Originally published in the *Chicago Sun-Times*, 1973.)

"THIS DAMN TEEPEE LEAKS."

"FRANKLY, IT'S THE LITTLE COMMIES I CAN'T STAND."

Richard Nixon, a famous anti-Communist going back to the days of HUAC and the Alger Hiss case in 1948, was the president who initiated détente with both the Soviet Union and China. Cuban dictator Fidel Castro hoped that Nixon would be open to lifting the U.S. embargo against his country, but new reports in March made clear that Nixon had no intention of thawing relations with the Communist island nation. (Originally published in the *Chicago Sun-Times,* 1974.)

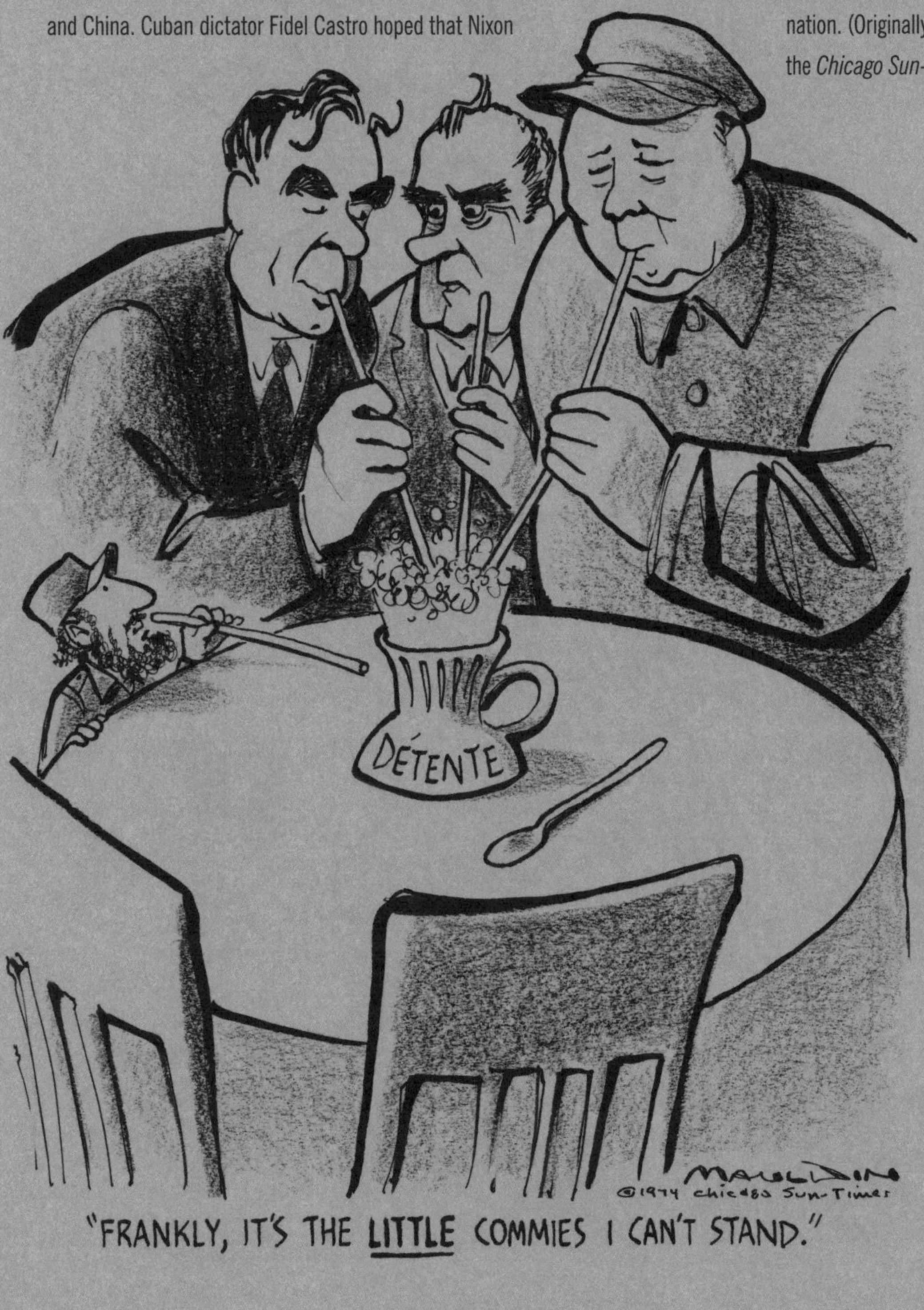
DÉTENTE
MAULDIN
©1974 Chicago Sun-Times

"FRANKLY, IT'S THE LITTLE COMMIES I CAN'T STAND."

RUSSIAN DÉTENTE, CHINESE DÉTENTE & NIXON ADMINISTRATION

(Originally published in the *Chicago Sun-Times,* 1974.)

UNTITLED [DEFENDING CIVIL LIBERTIES]

A strong proponent of civil rights and social justice campaigns throughout his lifetime, Mauldin illustrated here that those who advance reforms or policies are often the most unqualified to do so (Originally published in the *Chicago Sun-Times,* 1974.)

"...THIS ONE? IT'S A VACUUM HOSE FOR YOUR POCKET OR PURSE."

(Originally published in the *Chicago Sun-Times*, 1974.)

"...THIS ONE? IT'S A VACUUM HOSE FOR YOUR POCKET OR PURSE."

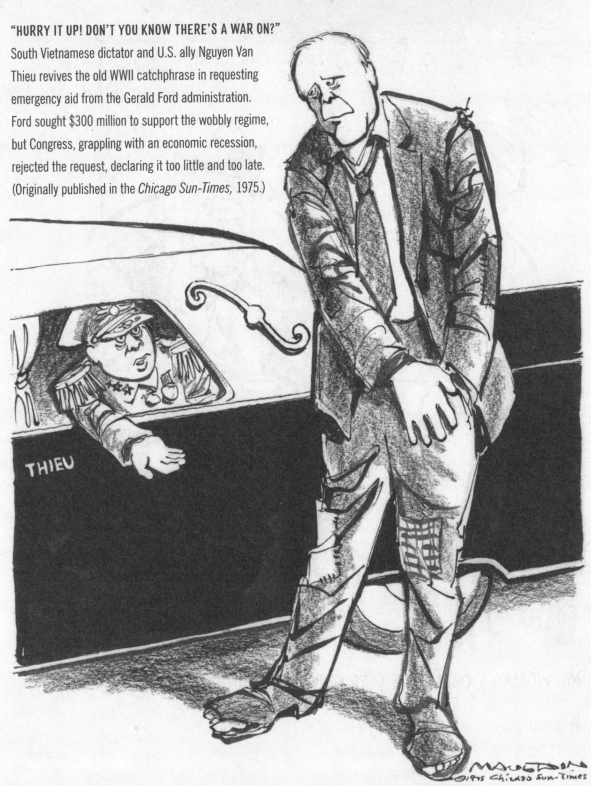

"HURRY IT UP! DON'T YOU KNOW THERE'S A WAR ON?"
South Vietnamese dictator and U.S. ally Nguyen Van Thieu revives the old WWII catchphrase in requesting emergency aid from the Gerald Ford administration. Ford sought $300 million to support the wobbly regime, but Congress, grappling with an economic recession, rejected the request, declaring it too little and too late. (Originally published in the *Chicago Sun-Times,* 1975.)

"HURRY IT UP! DON'T YOU KNOW THERE'S A WAR ON?"

"MY WOMAN'S OKAY. SHE SAYS SHE DON'T WANNA BE MY EQUAL."

"MY WOMAN'S OKAY. SHE SAYS SHE DON'T WANNA BE MY EQUAL."

Mauldin here recalls his own well-known cartoon from March 2, 1960, in which one southern white racist says to another during an attack on civil rights activists, "Let that one go. He says he don't wanna be mah equal." (Originally published in the *Chicago Sun-Times,* 1975.)

DOMINO THEORY
(Originally published in the
Chicago Sun-Times, 1975.)

DOMINO THEORY

©1975 Chicago Sun-Times

END OF THE BELT

This cartoon bookends Mauldin's coverage of the Vietnam War, mirroring one of his earliest cartoons on the subject from October 19, 1962. In that version, the same machine gun is being fed by rounds of soldiers, with a caption that reads, "Live Ammunition." (Originally published in the *Chicago Sun-Times,* 1975.)

END OF THE BELT

September 1975 saw two assassination attempts against President Gerald R. Ford. The first was by Squeaky Fromme, who pointed a Colt .45 at Ford in Sacramento on September 5 but didn't fire. The second was by Sara Jane Moore on September 22 in San Francisco. Moore fired two shots at Ford from close range but missed. (Originally published in the *Chicago Sun-Times*, 1975.)

"THIS TIME WE TOOK THE WHOLE CROWD INTO CUSTODY."

VALLEY FORGE

Mauldin spent years in the mid-1970s working on a cartoon history of the American Revolution. These drawings of Valley Forge scenes were intended for what would become *Mud and Guts: A Look at the Common Soldier of the American Revolution,* 1978.

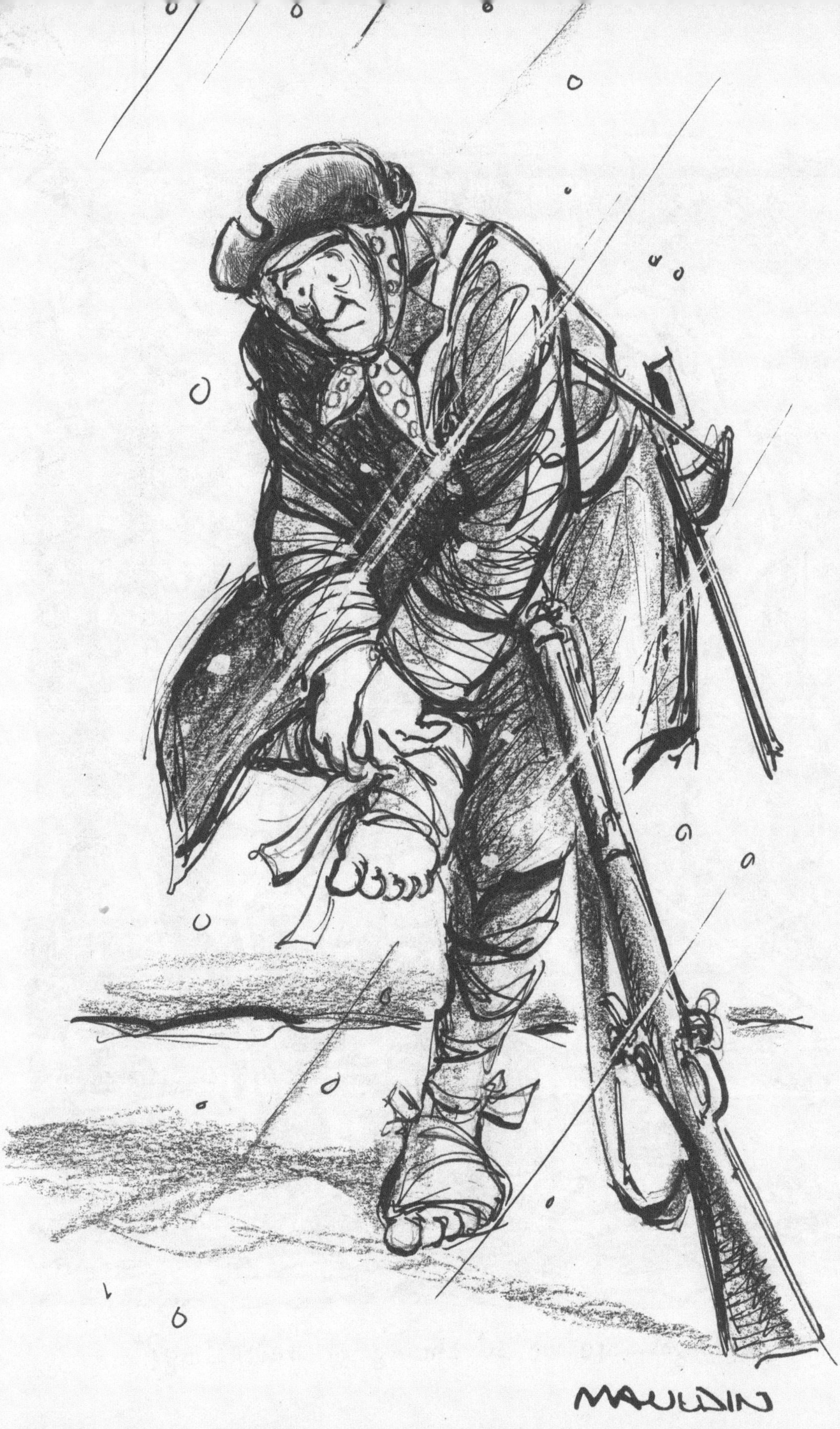
MAULDIN

"I forgot...are we advancing or retreating?"

"Now, that's what I call a complete revolution."

"NOW, THAT'S WHAT I CALL A COMPLETE REVOLUTION."
The Ayatollah Khomeini was the leader of the Iranian Revolution of 1979, which deposed the last Shah of Iran (Mohammad Reza Pahlavi) and created the Islamic Republic. Under Khomeini, things deemed too "Western" were eradicated, including women's rights, alcohol, music, and anything resembling political opposition. (Originally published in the *Chicago Sun-Times,* 1979.)

WINE

SONG

WOMEN

CRITICISM

©1979 Chicago Sun-Times

"HOW'D YOU LIKE
TO BE MEMBERS
OF A PERSECUTED
MAJORITY?"
(Originally published in the
Chicago Sun-Times, 1980.)

"How'd you like to be members of a persecuted <u>majority?</u>"

"THIS WAR OUGHT TO BE AFGHANISTANIZED."

"Vietnamization" was the name given by the Nixon administration to its strategy of turning the war over to the armed forces of South Vietnam, thereby reducing American involvement. At the end of 1979, the Soviet Union invaded Afghanistan to support a Communist government there. The invasion quickly bogged down in a brutal guerrilla war, much like the American war in Vietnam. (Originally published in the *Chicago Sun-Times,* 1980.)

"This war ought to be Afghanistanized."

KING OF THE CRAZIES

On November 4, 1979, Iranian revolutionaries stormed the U.S. embassy in Tehran and took more than fifty Americans hostage. The hostage standoff between the United States and Iran would end 444 days later, after the U.S. promised not to interfere in Iranian affairs and unfroze Iranian assets. (Originally published in the *Chicago Sun-Times,* 1980.)

King of the Crazies

"THIS'LL MAKE IT MORE SPORTING."

Republican presidential candidate Ronald Reagan ran an unapologetically conservative campaign against President Jimmy Carter in 1980. He opposed the Equal Rights Amendment (ERA) to the Constitution and supported a return to states' rights, which implied a turning away from federal commitments to civil rights. In the end, he split the women's vote evenly with Carter and lost the African American vote by almost seventy points. (Originally published in the *Chicago Sun-Times*, 1980.)

© 1980 Chicago Sun-Times

"This'll make it more sporting."

"I THOUGHT YOU MIGHT GET A KICK OUT OF IT."

"The Ransom of Red Chief" (1907) is a short story by O. Henry about two kidnappers who hold a wealthy boy hostage. The boy ends up driving the kidnappers crazy with his wild behavior, forcing the kidnappers to pay the father to take the kid back. (Originally published in the *Chicago Sun-Times,* 1980.)

©1980 Chicago Sun-Times

"I thought you might get a kick out of it."

"Let's declare ourselves winners and get the hell out."

RIGHT TO LIFE

Mauldin here takes the slogan from the antiabortion movement and applies it to children starving in the Uganda famine. (Originally published in the *Chicago Sun-Times*, 1981.)

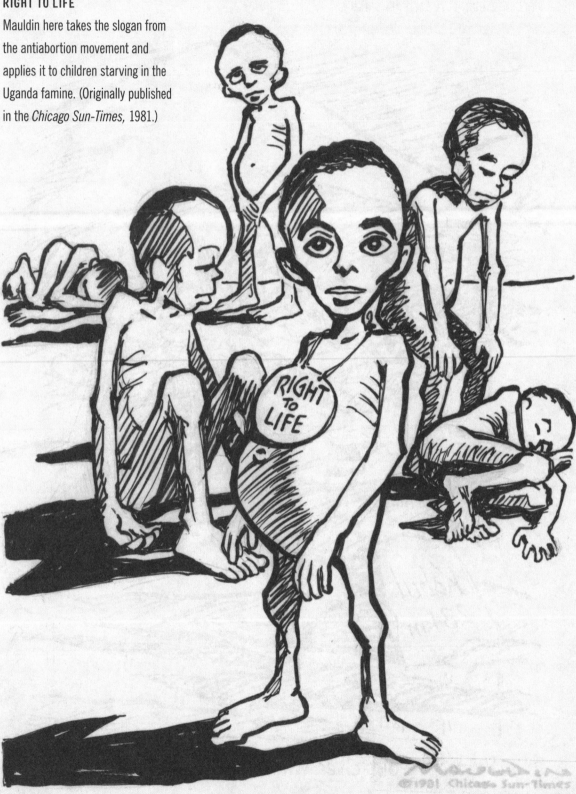

©1981 Chicago Sun-Times

"COME ON IN—THE QUICKSAND'S FINE."

During the Salvadoran Civil War of 1979 to 1992, the Reagan administration increased U.S. support for the military junta government fighting a left-wing insurgency. Observers like Mauldin feared a quagmire akin to the Soviet experience in Afghanistan. Mauldin references (or, perhaps, simply copies) a chilling cartoon by M. A. Kempf that appeared in *The Masses* in June 1917 during WWI. It shows the great powers of Europe dancing with death in a pool of blood. The caption reads, "Come on in, America, the blood's fine." (Originally published in the *Chicago Sun-Times,* 1982.)

"Come on in—the quicksand's fine."

"The good news is that there's plenty of mutton."

"← **"THE GOOD NEWS IS THAT THERE'S PLENTY OF MUTTON."**
On April 2, 1982, the Argentinian army invaded the Falkland Islands, a disputed British territory about 300 miles off Argentina's coast. The Falklands are desolate and sparsely populated, but Britain fought Argentina in a ten-week war to keep possession of them. (Originally published in the *Chicago Sun-Times*, 1982.)

"THE TRICK IS TO STAY BETWEEN THE HOBNAILS."
Solidarity was the name of an underground trade union founded in Communist Poland and led by Lech Walesa. It enjoyed enormous popular support. By some miracle, as well as international support and ingenious clandestine maneuvers, Solidarity managed to survive martial law and every other state effort to crush it. In 1989, the government finally relented and permitted open elections. (Originally published in the *Chicago Sun-Times*, 1984.)

SOLIDARITY

MAULDIN
©1984 Chicago Sun-Times

"The trick is to stay between the hobnails."

"Señor, without a chart how you gonna tell freedom fighters from terrorists?"

"SEÑOR, WITHOUT A CHART HOW YOU GONNA TELL FREEDOM FIGHTERS FROM TERRORISTS?"

The Reagan administration funneled aid to right-wing rebels in Nicaragua seeking to overthrow the Socialist "Sandinista" government. Throughout 1985 and 1986, Reagan referred to these "Contra" rebels as freedom fighters, while their opponents labeled them as terrorists for their atrocities against civilians and other political opponents. (Originally published in the *Chicago Sun-Times,* 1986.)

"OUTTA SIGHT, OUTTA MIND, HEY?"

Operation Desert Storm began on January 17, 1991, with an air campaign against Iraq. Seeking to roll back Iraq's annexation of neighboring Kuwait, a coalition force led by Americans and engineered by President George H. W. Bush then launched the second phase of the war, a land invasion of Kuwait and Iraq. This First Gulf War was short and decisive, leading to a U.S. victory. U.S. casualties were relatively low, reaching into the hundreds. (Originally published in the *Chicago Sun-Times,* 1991.)

The U.S. victory in the First Gulf War left Iraqi dictator Saddam Hussein in power and raised a number of questions about the United States' role in the region. Mauldin saw that despite President Bush's proclamation of victory, the Middle East was far from won. (Originally published in the *Chicago Sun-Times*, 1991.)

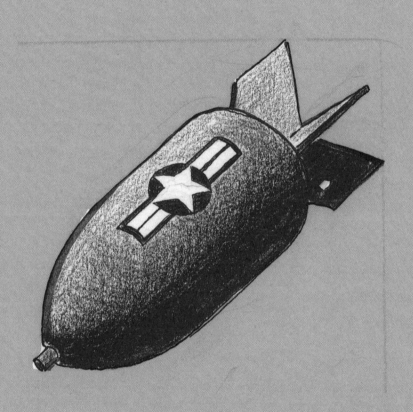

TOM BROKAW has spent his entire journalism career at NBC News, starting in 1966. He was the anchor of the *Today* show and anchor and managing editor of NBC Nightly News with Tom Brokaw. In 1988, he published the best-selling *The Greatest Generation*, the first of six books he has authored. Brokaw has won every major award in his craft and was awarded the Presidential Medal of Freedom by President Barack Obama in 2014.

TODD DEPASTINO is author of the award-winning *Bill Mauldin: A Life Up Front* and several other books. He holds a Ph.D. in history from Yale University and currently serves as executive director of the Veterans Breakfast Club, a 501(c)(3) nonprofit dedicated to sharing veterans' stories with the public.

TOM HANKS has received two Academy Awards for Best Actor. Other accolades include the Stanley Kubrick Britannia Award for Excellence in Film, the Kennedy Center Honors, the 2016 Presidential Medal of Honor, and the French Legion of Honor for his support of World War II veterans. His lead role in *Saving Private Ryan* and his work writing, directing, and producing the miniseries *Band of Brothers* were inspired by and deepened his appreciation of military service. He's proud to be an honorary member of the United States Army Rangers Hall of Fame.

CHRISTINA M. KNOPF holds a Ph.D. in Sociology and Communication from the University at Albany. She has been a college instructor of political rhetoric since 2001 and is currently an assistant professor in Communication and Media Studies at the State University of New York at Cortland. Dr. Knopf authored *The Comic Art of War: A Critical Study of Military Cartoons, 1805–2014*. She has also contributed essays to *Cultures of War in Graphic Novels: Violence, Trauma,* *and Memory* and *The 10 Cent War: Comic Books, Propaganda,* and *World War II.* She has spoken about representations of war in comics and cartoons at the San Diego Comic Con, the Goethe-Institut–Paris, the USS Constitution Museum, the Border Town Comic Con, and the Animation and Public Engagement Symposium, as well as at dozens of academic conferences.

DENISE NEIL is the executive director of the 45th Infantry Division Museum in Oklahoma City, which houses more than two hundred original Bill Mauldin World War II cartoons in its collection. She holds an M.A. degree from the University of New Mexico and an M.A. and Ph.D. from the University of Oklahoma. Her academic work has centered on visual culture and history, including her M.A. thesis, "Reflections of the Dogfaces: The World War II Cartoons of Bill Mauldin."

G. KURT PIEHLER is author of *Remembering War the American Way* and is currently writing a book on the religious life of the American GI in World War II. Piehler is the editor of the *Encyclopedia of Military Science* and *The United States in World War II: A Documentary Reader.* He also edits two book series, *World War II: The Global, Human, Ethical Dimension* and *Legacies of War.* He holds a Ph.D. in history from Rutgers University and is director of the Institute on World War II and the Human Experience at Florida State University.

JENNIFER N. PRITZKER is a retired Lieutenant Colonel of the United States Army who was promoted to the rank of honorary Colonel in the Illinois National Guard, a respected historian, entrepreneur, investor, and philanthropist. A veteran with a love of history, she founded the Pritzker Military Museum & Library in 2003 to promote and preserve the stories of the Citizen Solider and founded the TAWANI Foundation and Pritzker Military Foundation to promote both her personal and military philanthropic interests.

JEAN SCHULZ is the widow of Charles "Sparky" Schulz and founder and president of the board of directors at the Charles M. Schulz Museum.

CORD A. SCOTT holds a Ph.D. in American history from Loyola University Chicago and currently serves as a professor of history for the University of Maryland, Global Campus for Asia. He is the author of *Comics and Conflict* and *Four Colour Combat.* He has written for several encyclopedias and academic journals, such as the *International Journal of Comic Art,* the *Journal of Popular Culture,* and the *Journal of the Illinois State Historical Society,* and in several books on aspects of cultural history. His most recent work is on U.S. military cartoons in WWI, which was published in the journal *War, Literature & the Arts.* He resides in South Korea.

ACKNOWLEDGMENTS

Pritzker Military Museum & Library Board of Directors

Colonel (IL) J.N. Pritzker,

IL ARNG (Retired), Founder and Chair

Norman Bobins

Tyrone C. Fahner

Colonel Kevin W. Farrell, *Ph.D., U.S. Army (Retired)*

Lieutenant Commander Arie Friedman,

M.D., USNR-R (MC) (Retired)

Major General James Mukoyama, *U.S. Army (Retired)*

Mary Parthe

Susan Rifkin

John W. Rowe

Robert E. Sarazen

John H. Schwan

Captain John A. Williams, *Ph.D., USNR (Retired)*

Pritzker Military Museum & Library Staff

Rob Havers, *Ph.D., President & CEO*

Megan Williams, *Senior Director of External Affairs*

Roberto Bravo, *Director of Administration & Operations*

Dustin DePue, *Director of Museum Collections*

Teri Embrey, *Director of Library Services (Chief Librarian)*

Trevor Peterson, *Director of Development*

Martin Billheimer, *Library Clerk*

James Brundage, *Museum Curator*

Olivia Button, *Digital Collections Coordinator*

Leah Cohen, *Oral History & Reference Manager*

Mary Dickey, *Visitor Services & Sales Supervisor*

Luc Gourguechon, *Program & Marketing Coordinator*

ACKNOWLEDGMENTS

Paul Grasmehr, *Reference Coordinator*

Brad Guidera, *Production Manager*

Angela Kepler, *Mauldin Project Manager*

John LaPine, *Collections Services Manager*

Nathan Magnuson, *Administrative Assistant*

Andrea Martinez, *Archivist*

Tina Louise Mead, *Assistant Director of Library Services*

Angel Melendez, *Production Coordinator*

Javier Rangel, *Development & Membership Administrative Assistant*

Margaret Ruddy, *Special Collections Librarian*

Sarah Schwartz, *Marketing & Communications Manager*

Linda Sterling, *Assistant Director of Membership*

Katie Strandquist, *Assistant Director of Sales & Special Events*

The Drawing Fire Team

Colonel (IL) J. N. Pritzker, *IL ARNG (Retired), Contributor*

Todd DePastino, *Ph.D., Editor and Contributor*

Harriet Bell, *Managing Editor*

Scott Manning, *Marketing Editor*

Tom Brokaw, *Contributor*

Mary Casalino, *Assistant to Tom Brokaw*

Tom Hanks, *Contributor*

Allison Diamond, *Assistant to Tom Hanks*

Christina M. Knopf, *Ph.D., Contributor*

Denise Neil, *Ph.D., Contributor*

G. Kurt Piehler, *Ph.D., Contributor*

Jean Schulz, *Contributor*

Cord A. Scott, *Ph.D., Contributor*

Roberto de Vicq de Cumptich, *Cover & Book Designer*

Mark McCauslin, *Copy Editor*

Peter Grennen, *Proofreader*

Diana Meunier, *Production Coordinator*

Thérèse Shere, *Indexer*

Angela MacLean, Sam Goff, Jennifer Luickboldt and Gillie Colins, *Publishers Group West*

Nat Mauldin and the Mauldin Estate

Jonathan Gordon, Alston & Bird LLP

Betsy Grant, *Bvgrant Studios*

CF "Arik" Grant

Kent Bolke, *10th Mountain Division & Fort Drum Museum*

Steve Leonard, *Doctrine Man*

Wendy Pflug, *Billy Ireland Cartoon Library & Museum, The Ohio State University Libraries*

45th Infantry Division Museum

Library of Congress

Charles M. Schulz Museum

Marine Corps History Division

Stars and Stripes

TAWANI Enterprises, Inc.

The Pritzker Military Museum & Library [PMML] offers a world-class collection of resources on military history and affairs to the public. The mission of the PMML is to acquire and maintain an accessible collection of materials and to develop appropriate programs focusing on the citizen soldier in the preservation of democracy. The PMML makes available tens of thousands of books and veterans' resources through interlibrary loan. It uses artifacts, many donated by service members or their families, to create physical and online exhibits that tell the stories of service. The PMML is also home to the largest collection of Bill Mauldin's original cartoons. It broadcasts to millions the experiences and insights of authors, military leaders, scholars, and veterans through podcasts, television shows, and video. Explore the PMML's collections at: pritzkermilitary.org.

ABOUT THE PRITZKER MILITARY MUSEUM & LIBRARY◀

→INDEX←

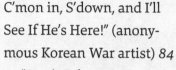

"Who Said My Medals Wouldn't Buy Me a Cuppa Coffee?" *124*

"Who's Winning––the Forces of Freedom or the People's Democracies?" *29*

➡ Y

"Yer a Menace to the People. It's Me Duty to Sink Your End of the Boat." *133*

"You Ain't Gaining Much Altitude Holding Me Down." *152*

"You First, Jack." *148*

"You Go Ahead an' Have a Good Time, Pop. I'm Too Tired." *55*

"Young Man, You've Got Nothing There But Weeds!" *157*

"You Soldiers Just Don't Seem to Understand Our Problems." *58*

DRAWING FIRE